GROWTH THROUGH GROUPS

William Clemmons and
Harvey Hester

Introduction by Findley B. Edge

BROADMAN PRESS
Nashville, Tennessee

Library of Congress Catalog Card Number: 74-77359
Dewey Decimal Classification: 301.18
Printed in the United States of America

Dedicated

to

Bettie and Yvonne,

who have affirmed us in

risking the new that God is creating,

even when it wasn't too clear

what the new might look like

nor where it might lead,

and to

all those who, in small groups,

have been our teachers

CONTENTS

Preface   ix

Introduction   13

1   A Cup Tells the Tale   25

2   Lonely, Hungry People   30

3   Small Groups in the Church—
     Feeding Hungry People   40

4   Sharing Groups—Growth in *Koinonia*   51

5   Sharing Groups—Growth in
     Personal Depth   61

6   How to Get Started   85

7   This Is the Way We Grow—Struggle   95

8   Understanding the Dynamics
     of Small Groups   102

9   Support for Mission—"AMBEK"   113

10   Mission Groups—Growth in Mission   122

11   Small Groups—Alternative
     Structures in the Church   145

Suggestions for Further Reading   158

PREFACE

This book is the work of two persons who share the same concern about the renewal of Christians and the churches of which they are part. We wish to see a new vitality emerge within those persons who have committed their lives to Christ and within those communities of faith where small groups have emerged as new expressions of those "called out" to be God's new people.

We want to see caterpillars emerge from cocoons of self-defeating behavior and become butterflies that can soar in the Spirit; lions, who lost their freedom in cages of despair, emerge and roar once more; elephants, once chained to their fears, roam the forests again; and eagles, who have been earthbound, soar as before.

Though we have written separately and together, we have written with only one editorial "I." Much of one person's experiences have been the other's, and there was no way to separate one person's experiences from the other's.

We have not attempted to present a book of research on small groups; there are other sources for that. Nor, is this a book on the psychological basis for small groups; there are also many excellent works available for those who wish to pursue that valuable study. We have not addressed ourselves to the use of the small group format as another technique in the educational program (buzz groups, etc.). Nor do we tell how to make committees and other task groups more efficient through an understanding of group process.

What we have tried to do is to make a basic statement about the use of the small group in the ongoing life of the church as a means for life-style change in persons and churches. *Growth Through Groups* is a statement of how personal and congregational growth can occur in three areas of life: growth in *koinonia;* growth in depth; and growth in mission. Because these are fundamental to a personal understanding of God's call to be his people, and its corporate fulfillment in the local church, this book seeks to speak to the development of a new personal and corporate lifestyle.

Actually, we are speaking to a process of growth; a journey into a life-style that can be summed up in the words "free to fulfill my Christian potential." This phrase applies both to personal Christian living and to the church's nature (fellowship) and purpose (mission). It is a costly pilgrimage involved in Christian potential, but it is one that is rich with promise.

We have attempted to examine these dimensions of growth through the use of three "alternative structures" which a church can create alongside existing church educational organizations: sharing groups, an indepth study structure, and mission groups. The book explores growth by starting where people are hungry for a sense of meaning and belonging. It then examines this hunger in the church and the possibility of the church using small groups to meet this need. Since growth is a process, the entrance point for people who are searching is first in "sharing groups." Then, they are introduced to the "indepth study structures," and finally to "mission groups." Three case studies are presented to provide illustrations of small groups in a local church setting and at different stages of group development. In the last chapter, we have discussed these alternative structures as coexisting in the life of the church alongside existing structures as a way of dealing effectively with both personal and structural renewal in the church.

Though we accept the responsibility for our own interpretations of small groups in the church, we do recognize the invaluable leadership of those who have plowed this ground before us, and through their conferences and books have given us our greatest insight into the understanding of the specialized role of small groups in the church setting: Gordon Cosby, Elizabeth O'Connor, Lyman Coleman, Keith Miller, Bruce Larson, Ralph Osborne, Findley Edge, George Kinnamon, Ben Johnson, David Haney, and Larry Richards.

We also acknowledge with deep gratefulness some individuals

and churches without whose help this book would have been the poorer: to a group of lay people in the 1950's at Tusculum Hills Baptist Church, Nashville, Tennessee, who first taught a struggling young minister the biblical teaching of the ministry of the laity through their leadership responsibility in building a new congregation; to a group of people in the Beechwood Baptist Church, Louisville, Kentucky, who, as part of a "strugglers class," became the first small group of my experience; to Rev. Richard Smith and others of the Glendale Baptist Church, Nashville, Tennessee, who participated in a task force for nine months in which some of these understandings about renewal were affirmed; to Reid Hardin and James Johnson for their guidance of "religious professionals" by letting us experience lay-led weekends with lay people leading small groups; to Rev. Jim Daniel of the Church of the Covenant, Louisville, Kentucky, whose insights opened up new dimensions of the church in the areas of gifts, mission, and community; to Rev. Joe Williams of Baptist Tabernacle, Louisville, Kentucky, who as colleague and friend, not only modeled sustained ministry to the brokenness of society for me, but was the first to indicate to me some directions for the healing of black/white relationships; to Lyman Coleman, whose personal "serendipity" has been both encourager and wise guide in how to build lasting interpersonal relationships; to Gordon Cosby, who has been a resource leader five times at The Vineyard since the beginning of Church Renewal Conferences here in Louisville in 1964, and who each time has pointed the way to the deeper dimensions of small mission groups; to Findley Edge, who not only as our teacher, colleague and friend was gracious enough to write the introduction, but has been willing to trust the "tending of the grapes" at The Vineyard to two guys like us; and finally to Nancy Chen and Bonnie Hicks for typing the manuscript.

William Clemmons
Harvey Hester

The Vineyard
Louisville, Kentucky

INTRODUCTION

In the last two decades, literally thousands of Christians have found a deeper sense of the reality and the power of God in their lives through experiences in small groups. The explosion of small groups across the United States among people of all religious persuasions has been nothing short of phenomenal. This development is all the more remarkable when one considers that there were no denominations that consciously sought to promote it.

The emergence of the small group on the current scene was a spontaneous phenomenon in which one, whose life was enriched by this experience, shared with another what was happening in his life. In this manner the movement has spread like wildfire across our nation. Why has the small group experience emerged and grown so rapidly at this particular time? Some of us believe that the Holy Spirit of God has been in it giving leadership, direction, and power.

Impersonal Society

Undoubtedly, there have been other factors, both in society and in the religious situation within the churches, that have called forth the small group and created the climate in which it has flourished. One of these factors is the increasing impersonalization of modern society. Someone has pointed out that the closer human beings have come together physically in modern society, the farther apart they have become emotionally and relationally.

For example, my grandfather lived on a farm in North Georgia. His closest neighbors lived several miles away, and having only a horse and wagon as a means of travel, it took considerable time and effort to see even one's closest neighbor. However, when I heard my grandfather speak of his neighbors, he spoke of them in the most intimate terms. Although these people were separated by considerable time and distance, they were exceedingly close relationally. When there was a death in one of the families, all the neighbors came from miles around to bring food, and also to bring love and support for the family in this time of crisis. If the farmer became ill during the time of harvest, all the neighbors would "pitch in" to help harvest the crop. If a barn burned down, then all the neighbors would come together for a "barn raising." That generation in their life-style was rather widely separated in time and distance, but relationally they were exceedingly close. "My neighbor" meant something then.

Today, however, in our urban setting with our urban life-style, we are exceedingly close physically, but we are miles apart emotionally and relationally. In our cities with their bumper-to-bumper traffic, with office and apartment buildings towering overhead seemingly about to engulf all that is below, we are like worms in a can, crawling all over each other but never touching one another. A family in a high-rise apartment scarcely knows the family living in the next apartment and certainly does not know (and does not care to know) the ones who live on the floor above or below. And, so we move closer to a society in which we are just a number. But eventually our very nature rebels against this. We were not made to be a number; we were made for community. Thus, in a society that is becoming increasingly impersonal, the small group provides a setting in which I can be a *human* being in relationship and not merely an animal who simply exists. I can know and be known. I can love and be loved.

Impersonal Religion

Society is not the only thing that has become impersonal. Religion, also, has tended to become impersonal for too many of us. There are some things in our religious practice which, in and of themselves, are good. However, when these things are overemphasized or when they are magnified to the exclusion of something else, then they become a problem for us. For example, it is highly desirable, indeed imperative, that the Christian faith be taught to all age groups in our churches. However, we are faced with a serious spiritual problem if and when this teaching and learning becomes primarily conceptual in nature.

Christianity is certainly a rational faith. It goes beyond the rational but it has a rational base. As such, Christianity, in part consists of, and is concerned with, concepts and ideas. The danger is that our religion may come to consist primarily of concepts and ideas we say we believe rather than a deep personal relationship with Christ. A person may believe all the correct doctrines which his particular denomination holds without this personal relationship. A person may engage in a lively discussion of the question, "What did Paul teach about faith?" But this question deals primarily with a concept; it says absolutely nothing about one's personal struggle with faith and doubt. The individual may be embarrassed because he has these questions and nagging doubts about various aspects of the Christian faith. He feels guilty because he has them (since no one else seems to have them), so he keeps his personal struggle well hidden and deals only with generalized concepts. He may discuss the teachings of Jesus, the miracles of Jesus—all concepts—without confronting in any serious way his personal relationship with Jesus.

Thus, one of the weaknesses of the teaching and learning that takes place in our Sunday Schools is that so much of it tends to be conceptual in nature. We simply play verbal volleyball, batting words back and forth to each other, or batting concepts and ideas "across the net." We may discuss how wonderful Hosea's attitude was toward Gomer, his wife; consider the problem involved in Jacob's deception of his father, Isaac; reflect upon Moses' experience at the burning bush. We can consider all of these, in a highly vocal manner, without ever considering in any serious way where we are in terms of our personal relationships with Jesus Christ. In a small group an individual becomes personal. He may be studying the Bible, but he does so, not in a conceptual manner, but in personal terms. "This is where I am." "Here is where I hurt." "This is the point where I really am having a struggle." The small group has built such an intimate relationship and such a deep level of trust that the individual feels safe to reveal the deeper levels of his struggle which he does not dare share in other groups where there are only superficial relationships.

Incarnation

The theological justification for the use of small groups in our churches is based on the doctrine of incarnation. One of the deep needs of our time is for our Christian faith to become more "alive" within us; to become more "real" and more "personal." Many in our churches who have been members most of their lives, who even have held leadership responsibilities, too often only routinely go through the forms of our religious life, singing the hymns, praying the prayers, going to meetings without any real sense of excitement about the Christian faith. Then, in some way they become a member of a small group. Out of this searching, sharing, and praying together, suddenly their Christian faith takes on a new dimension, a new depth! Their walk with Christ becomes much more personal and exciting! How did this happen?

This is where the doctrine of incarnation comes into focus. In biblical times God spoke to his people in a variety of ways, but this was always limited. His clearest Word to us was through his Son. "In many and various ways God spoke of old to our fathers by the prophets; but in these last days he has spoken to us by a Son" (Heb. 1:1-2, RSV). The highest revelation of God is through incarnation. We came to know what God was really like in terms of his love and forgiveness (and in all the other characteristics of his being). He became incarnate in Jesus Christ. "And The Word became flesh and dwelt among us" (John 1:14, RSV). Today, through his Holy Spirit, God still comes to us in many ways. He comes to us through the Scriptures, through private meditations, through preaching, and in other ways.

Still one of the most effective ways by which the Holy Spirit speaks to us is through an incarnation in another person. We come to understand and experience the love of God more clearly because we experience God's love in another person. We come to understand how it is that God can know all there is about us and yet love us and accept us as we are, because in a small group some other people have come to know us as we really are and have loved and accepted us as we are.

The Holy Spirit uses other persons to meditate the reality of God to us. I know this to be true in my own experience. It happened when I must have been somewhere close to forty years old. I had been a Christian for many years. I am sure I had known and had experienced something of the love of God. I had studied about God's love and had heard sermons preached about it. In fact, I had preached sermons about it. But it was not until I became a part of a small group that all of this took on a whole new perspective for me. That which before had tended to be theoretical and abstract began to be real. There were no dramatic or highly emotional experiences connected with this. The fact is that while the group was meeting I was not even aware that anything was happening to me.

It was not until I looked back over those experiences of a few months that I realized something rather profound had taken place in my life. For one thing I came to be aware in a deeper way than I had ever known before of God's love for me and his acceptance of me as I was (though always desiring better things for me). The people in that small group knew me as I was with my failures, my weaknesses, my struggles, and yet they loved me. This was a rather overwhelming experience for me because I had always lived my life (as evidently many people do) with the feeling that if people knew me as I really was they would not like me. So I spent so much of my time trying to hide the "real me" from people and present to them a "me" I felt they would like. But these people knew me as I was (or at least a lot better than anyone had ever known me before) and yet they still loved me. It was through this type of relationship that I became more deeply aware that God, who knew me as I was, could also love me. God through his Holy Spirit used other people—"incarnation"—to reveal himself to me.

There is a reverse side of the experience also. Not only did I come to know at a deeper level what it meant to be loved, I also came to know, through "incarnation," what it meant to love others. Because of the searching, sharing, praying we did together, because of the relationships we experienced together, I came to love the members of this group in a way I had never loved people before, outside of my immediate family. I really came to know these people. I knew where they ached. I knew where they struggled. I knew their deep yearnings. I knew the particular points where they were striving to change and to grow.

I prayed daily for each one of them by name. And because I knew them I loved them. In the seminary I learned what: *koinonia* (fellowship, community) meant. That is, I learned it at a conceptual level. And I am sure I experienced it on a certain level in my life in the church. But it was with this group, in relationship—"incarnation"—that I came closer to experiencing what I think New Testament *koinonia* is like than ever before in my life. Unfortunately this kind of experience is rare rather than usual for many of us.

But someone may object that it is precisely this kind of close relationship among its members that causes it to become a clique. My initial reaction to this objection is simply to say that I think I had rather have some cliques in my church where the participants really love each other, than to have the usual kind of church fellowship where we slap each other on the back, drink punch together, carry on casual conversation, but do not care for one another on any depth level. But let me not treat this objection lightly. It is true that a small group does face the danger of becoming introverted, of caring so much for the members of the group they seemingly care for no one else. Those who participate in small groups must be aware of this danger and avoid it with diligence. However, this was not the case with me. So far as I am able to understand myself, I feel that because of my relationship with the members of this group I came to love God more deeply than I ever had before, and I came to have a love for other people that was deeper than I had known before. All of this simply illustrates that God still uses incarnation—other people—as a primary means for revealing himself to men.

Some Values

When one says that small groups may be an aid in helping people meet God at a deeper level in their lives and helping their Christian faith become more alive, more real, and more personal, what more needs to be said? There are other values, however, that may come from this relationship. For one thing we come to have the feeling that there really can be a group who cares for us and cares for us deeply. My experience would indicate that many people, maybe most, have a poor self image.

When we are honest with ourselves, many of us have to admit that we have some rather serious doubts about ourselves and our abilities. Other people appear to us to "have it all together." They seem so confident and sure of themselves. But we are so aware of our weaknesses. This is another way of saying we really don't like ourselves (which is contrary to Jesus' teaching). Because we don't like ourselves we have the feeling that other people don't like us either. In a small group through the quality of the relationships, the group says to each member: "I really like you. I care for you deeply."

Another value that comes to most individuals as the result of being a part of this type of caring fellowship is they come to believe more deeply in themselves and in their power to become. This is due in part to the fact that they begin to like themselves better. It is due in part to the work of the Holy Spirit who helps them become aware that through Christ "all things can become new." Although they are deeply aware of their own weaknesses and failings, in this community where people care, they become more keenly aware of the Power that enables them to become increasingly the creation God intends for them to be. And so with this assurance, they begin to become, to change, to grow. Many have found that as a part of a group, they are much more willing to change some aspect of their lives or risk some difficult undertaking. In the group they have both encouragement and support. They also know that if they fail, as often they will, the group still loves and will pick them up, bind up any wounds, and encourage them to try again. In this type of relationship many have found the inner courage, the spiritual strength, and the human support to break out of the cocoon in which their lives have been bound and experience the freedom and joy of becoming a beautiful butterfly.

On the other hand the group experience does not consist only of "sweetness and light." The group members minister to each other by holding each other accountable. Yet this does not inject a dark factor into group life. It must be understood that accountability in reality is an expression of love. It simply means that I simply will not let you be less than the best God wants you to be. It means that if you have caught a vision of the "self"

God wants you to become in some area of your life, I will not let you quit after only a couple of weeks of trying. If you have heard God's call to some daring and worthy ministry, I will not let you "goof off." I will hold you accountable. It will be done in love but love holds you accountable. Genuine love wants you to fulfill your potential in your life. Love wants you to fulfill your calling and ministry under God.

Small Groups and Churches

When small groups first began to emerge, many pastors rejected them for a variety of reasons, some of which were valid, some of which were based on misunderstandings. Some identified these groups with sensitivity training and the bizarre happenings related to this movement reported by a variety of news media. Others heard of the weird approaches used by some encounter groups and the psychological damage that was done to some who participated in these experiences. Others saw these groups as being completely humanistic in their approach and emphasis.

In the beginning most of these groups grew up outside the churches, even those groups that were completely spiritually oriented and Bible based. Generally they were composed of those who had a certain disillusionment with what was happening (or not happening) in the churches. They met in some home during the week. Because the participants were unhappy over the life of the church, the reports that got back to the pastor and other church leaders was that the major thing being done in these groups was to criticize the church and the pastor. Whether or not this was true undoubtedly varied with different groups. However, irrespective of what actually went on within the groups, the *report* was this was a "I hate the church" type of group. Thus, it is easy to see how pastors viewing these groups from this perspective vigorously rejected these "negative" groups.

Another criticism often leveled against these groups was that the participants tended to become a bunch of "super-pious, self-righteous, Holy Joes." They were accused of developing a spiritual pride and expressing a spiritual snobbery that alienated them completely from the rest of the church members. It must be confessed that too often this was the impression given to other people by small group participants. On the other hand a great deal of this impression was based on a misunderstanding. Most of these people did not feel either "super-pious" or "self-righteous." Rather it was exactly the opposite. They were keenly aware of their failures, their shortcomings, their struggles. In their struggle and search within the group, they began to make some discoveries. God became more real and more personal. They became excited about some of the things they were discovering. They simply wanted to share what was happening to them. But when they shared, others tended to feel they were expressing a "holier than thou" attitude. And so alienation occurred among Christians when that which was happening should have been a unifying experience and an occasion for rejoicing.

Another question often asked relative to small groups and the church concerned the fact that there are already small groups in the church in the form of Sunday School classes, training groups, men's and women's groups. So, why do we need other small groups? This is a good question and deserves a serious answer. The small groups we now have, such as Sunday School classes and the other educational organizations, serve a very useful function in education *and* outreach. Both of these functions are important and necessary emphases in the life of the churches. However, one major difference between these small groups in the church and the small groups about which this book is concerned is the depth and quality of the relationships among the participants. Because one of the major purposes of the present classes and other groupings within our churches is outreach, new people are constantly being brought into the class. As a result, although we have a relationship within these organizations, and although there is expressed in them a caring—often of a meaningful type especially in times of illness—yet as a general rule we do not share the deep areas of our struggles with these people.

We do not share the depths of our lives until we have built a rather deep, trusting relationship. It takes time to build this type of relationship. *Every time you add a new person to that group, you change the climate of that group.* This certainly is not to say that we do not need groups where we can bring in new people. It simply means we need *one* group where we do

not constantly add new people; a place where I can share and
search and struggle and pray concerning some of the deeper levels
of my life which I simply am unwilling to share with just any
group.

In our churches we speak so often of "community" as though
it were something relatively easy to achieve. However such is
not the case. We seek to build "Christian community" through
fellowships and socials, and although these may have helped build
some relationships, these do not get at the basic matter of community. Community is simply not relationships in which we are in
close physical proximity with other people, such as in a worship
service or at a social gathering. Community is a *quality* of relationships. The number of people with whom we can be related
casually in a particular grouping can be quite large. However,
the number of people with whom we can be "in community"
is necessarily small. It is a relationship in which I can come to
be known and be known in depth. This level of relationship cannot
be achieved if new people are constantly being brought into the
group. Just as we need groups in the church where new people
can be assimilated, we also need groups in the church where we
can experience deeper relationships.

The strong emphasis being given here to small groups is not
to suggest that they are the panacea for all of the ills of the
church. Not everyone who participates in a small group will
experience this deeper relation with God which I have been
describing. There is no magical formula connected with small
groups. Also it should be clearly stated that small groups are not
for everyone in the church. Some find the small groups threatening.
Others, for a variety of valid reasons, would find them not desirable.

However, recent experience has indicated that the small group
is one channel which God has used to enable many thousands
of persons to come into a deeper, more personal relationship with
him. For this reason churches need to make use of these small
groups as a part of their regular life.

Dr. William Clemmons and Dr. Harvey Hester, co-directors
of The Vineyard Conference Center, have written this book to
meet this specific need of deepening the lives of persons and

churches through the use of small groups. Their approach is personal, positive, and practical. They are eminently qualified for this task, both by virtue of their academic training and their experience. Through reading this book I hope you will be stimulated to participate in a small group; and if you do, my prayer is that it will be a deeply meaningful spiritual experience as you are opened to new areas of personal Christian growth.

Findley B. Edge

Southern Baptist Theological Seminary
Louisville, Kentucky

1 A Cup Tells the Tale

Ten people were sitting on the floor of the pastor's home after the evening services. It looked like an ordinary group in many ways, but their purpose was different from many other gatherings of couples on Sunday evenings for a brief time of informal socializing. They had come at the invitation of the pastor to participate in a small group experience.

It had all begun several weeks earlier when the pastor and his wife and two other couples had participated at a nearby church as a group of resource persons in a lay renewal weekend. Small groups had been part of the activities during the weekend. This sparked an interest among the six people, and the question was asked, "Why don't we begin a small group in our church?"

The group in the pastor's home was as diverse in background as it was in their interest in being there. But there they were, not sitting in chairs as was the usual custom and balancing a plate of cookies and punch on one knee while trying to carry on some kind of conversation with the person next to them who was just as uncomfortable as they were about the whole "fellowship thing." Instead, this group found itself sitting on the floor and some had even removed their shoes in an attempt at casualness, though a certain undercurrent of nervousness about it was very apparent.

After a few minutes of false starts and stops at conversation—for this group did not normally socialize together—one of the group suggested that we (I was a member of the group) go around the group and introduce ourselves, but not in the usual fashion of name, rank, and serial number (which in church language is translated as name, occupation, and number of children). The way we were to do it was by pulling out two things we had on our person either out of our pockets or purses: one that would represent something "outstanding or unique" about us, and one that would represent an area in which we would like to experience growth.

As I sat there trying to outfumble everyone else as I rummaged through my pockets, I kept thinking to myself: How did I let myself get talked into this by my wife? This is the stupidist thing I've ever seen grown persons do. If they wanted to play parlor games why didn't they say so; at least we could have been sitting at a game table where the rules were clear to everybody.

Finally I came up with two things, but I was surely glad that I wasn't the first to lead off. One of the wives, who had suggested this procedure in the first place, began to share her two items.

She pulled out of her purse first a piece of peppermint candy and said: "This represents my good humor. I think that is the one thing that I would say about myself that is most characteristic of me. At least people say I always am looking at the funny and humorous things in a situation. So this peppermint candy stands for my good humor."

The group around her burst into a nervous kind of laughter, but in a real way I could tell that this was true about Bettie. Somehow she always was the one to see the humorous and to keep people laughing with her way of telling a story or recounting the latest event in the neighborhood.

Then, a little more slowly she picked up the second item. "This is my checkbook, and I could just as well have picked up the little case that has my credit cards in it, for this is the place I need to grow as much as anywhere else in my life—learning how to manage money."

With these words there was a little nervous shifting of positions and even a few attempts at smoothing over this confession of growth by saying, "Yeah, I could use some help there too!" But there was a realization also that a truth had been spoken which had not been demanded or painfully pulled out of a person. It was just a simple statement of need.

The next hour was spent just like that, for it took about five minutes apiece to say two simple things about ourselves. Yet, they really weren't simple when you were the next to speak. I could feel the resistance grow in me, and yet there was a liberation too as I pulled out my comb and said that the most unique thing about me was the comb I carried to comb the hair that grows only "on the sides of my head. I don't have to spend time combing as much as other people do!" But the second item was really at my gut level as I pulled out the little plastic container with my tranquilizers in it and said that I need to learn to manage the tensions inside me.

Within an hour I knew more about persons I thought I had had a good acquaintance with over the past three years in that church than I had known about my closest working associates. The things that people pulled out of their pockets and purses, both to tell me of their strengths and where they knew they needed to grow, made up the most honest and open conversation I had had with anyone in years. Small pocket Bibles became confessions of doubt and ignorance about what was involved in the "Christian game"; pocket knives became symbols of pent-up hatred; pictures of relatives were representations of grief experiences which had never been resolved. Over and over again the four housewives, the salesman, the high-school teacher, the farmer, the dentist, the real estate agent, and the pastor talked. We talked not of the abstract and conceptual things that are found in most conversations so that the level of conversation never gets "too personal," but we talked of ways in which we found things we liked about ourselves, as well as the areas in which we were too painfully aware that we needed to mature.

All of us felt foolish at first and resisted the game approach, but we soon found that what appeared to be a game was really a structure to talk about what each one of us had wanted to talk about to an understanding person for a long time. After an hour, there was a closeness that bound us together, for sharing and community had been experienced at a deeper level.

After a stand-up break and the passing around of coffee and cookies, we continued in the circle. Again, Mary Jo started us off, but this time the instructions were to take a paper cup, let it represent the church, and then do with it what we would. As she told us what to do she explained that this was a good way for us to allow feelings to be a part of what we were trying to say by using a tangible object toward which to express those feelings. We were all to be silent; and after we had done whatever we wanted to with the cup, expressing what we would like to see the church be and become, we were to pass it silently on to the next person. The cup was to be passed around the circle as many times as we wanted until everyone was satisfied with what had been done to the cup. Then we were to break the silence and share what we felt about what had happened.

Well, the first person took the cup up in her arms and hugged it and passed it on. The next person, Bill, the dentist took it and carefully tore window-like holes in it. Jim, the farmer, took it and carefully took the pieces that Bill had torn out for the windows and distributed them to each member in the circle. By the time all ten of the group had taken the cup on the first round, the cup had been torn open, flattened out, pieces shared with each person, and a cross made of other pieces.

The second and third passing of the pieces of the cup saw other things done with the cup as each person tried to express what they were feeling about the church, taking it in the condition it had just been given to him or her each time. After about fifteen minutes of this, the group finally felt that all were satisfied and the discussion began.

"Bill, after you had torn holes in the cup, why did you then stomp on it the second time around?" asked Alice. "That seemed to be the most irreverent thing that could have been done."

Then, there came out a story of hostility towards the church for its smugness and hypocrisy in a recent confrontation between blacks and whites in which the church had remained out of the issue because of a belief that politics and religion don't mix.

"Yet," Alice replied, "you tore holes in the cup the first time around. Why?"

"Because, that's what I hope can happen. I would like to see some windows of our church thrown open so that a new wind could blow through it and a renewal take place. I would like to see the Holy Spirit allowed to come into our church and old things made new; new wineskins made for a fermenting wine that can really make a difference in the lives of Christians. But, when all of you just kept playing around with the cup like you do at church, hugging it, lifting it up as if it was untouchable, and trying to smooth out the rough edges, I just stomped it for I felt like that was what God was going to do if we didn't get with it."

More honesty about the possibilities and failures of our church came out of that night than I had heard in tons of church business meetings, bushels of deacon's meetings, and barrels of official conferences. Why? Because a few people had tried to be open, honest, caring, and vulnerable for an hour and a half sitting on a living room floor in the pastor's home. And, a small group provided the means by which it had all happened.

2 Lonely, Hungry People

When persons are asked how they really feel about themselves, the church, or their Christian experience, both hope and failure are found in the answers of most people. There is a sense of failure and the need for change, but there is also hope because God seems to be pointing the way through thousands of persons to the new signs of his renewing work. Wherever people are gathering together in small sharing and mission groups, these new dimensions of growth are being experienced and discussed, and new life is taking place, both in persons, and in the churches of which they are part.

A Deep Hunger in Society Today

Any examination of the hunger that is evident among God's people must first be explored in the society in which persons live and the church exists. Part of the cause of that hunger is found in a hunger of the times in which we live. This hunger has been pointed to by many writers during the past few years, including Charles Reich, who has described this hunger that pervades much of American life as a feeling of the lost, impoverished self. He says that the true self is lost by the pressure to conform and the subsequent loss of the "freedom to be." The end product is a person who has "good character," in that he has never violated any laws, is not rebellious against the authority structures, and is a team person who goes along with the others. But, this kind of existence ends up producing a "hollow man" who is alienated from meaningful work, a real self, and the real need of being a person. Instead, modern men "have surrounded themselves by things, and rendered themselves passive in the process; it is as if they have given up the power to change and grow and create, and things have acquired this power instead; things change and dance, and the individual sits motionless, besotted, and empty. For he who can neither act to fulfill his own genuine needs, nor act to help his society in its dire need, has no genuine existence." [1]

Alvin Toffler has also described this hunger in modern man, but in slightly different terms. He sees today's man as the "modular man." He can be "plugged in" and "plugged out" at random and moved about as a nomad. This has resulted in "limited relationships" which are neither deep nor lasting. This, according to Toffler, is the way modern man has adjusted both to the mobile society of which he is part and to the increase in the very number of persons with which he comes into contact every day. Therefore, the majority of these relationships tend to be temporary and superficial. Only family relationships become in any sense "long-duration relationships," though these too are often revived only at special occasions since most modern Americans live the one-generational type family existence with parents and brothers and sisters living in other areas of the nation. Those relationships which Toffler classifies as of medium-duration are friendships, neighborhood relationships, on-the-job relationships, and membership relationships. Lastly, there are the short-duration relationships which usually involve those in service-related occupations; the sales clerk who waits on us, and the cashier at the grocery. Thus, a pattern of life has grown up in this nation in which "rather than becoming deeply involved with the total personality of every individual we meet . . . we necessarily maintain superficial and partial contact with some." Also, the more mobile a person is, "the greater the number of brief, face-to-face encounters, human contacts, each one a relationship of sorts, fragmentary and above all, compressed in time." [2]

Another author examined this same aspect of hunger in modern man, but from the point of view of community. Vance Packard, in a book entitled, *A Nation of Strangers,* has called us a "society of torn roots." He points out the cause for this type of society is found in the high mobility rate with which we have lived for the past few decades. He said he came to believe "that at least forty million Americans now lead feebly-rooted lives. We are seeing so deep an upheaval of life patterns that we are becoming a nation of strangers." Packard attributed this rootlessness to five causes: people constantly on the move; the flight to the suburbs from stable inner-city neighborhoods; the rise of multiple-dwelling high-rise units; small towns where plants and factories employ people on an around-the-clock shift basis; and the breakup of the multi-generational family unit.[3]

Finally, one other analysis of the hunger is found in William Glasser's book, *The Identity Society*. He identifies the source of today's hunger as coming from a major cultural shift from a goal-directed society to a role-or identity-motivated society. As he examined students in public schools, he concluded that they were "reaching for a role, an identity, a human condition that we have thought little about in our struggle to reach a goal . . . recently something new has happened, that the struggle for a goal—a profession, a diploma, a home, a family—has been super-seded by the struggle to find oneself as a human being, to become aware and enjoy the pleasures implicit in our own humanity. . . . Role, or identity, is now so important that it must be achieved before we set out to find a goal. We can no longer afford to ignore this new priority in human motivation." [4]

Thus, four writers have described a basic hunger that exists in American society resulting from a loss of identity, mobility, rootlessness, and a longing for identity. Another writer, though he has also underlined these same causes for a basic hunger in our society, has also pointed to some possible sources of help.

Sidney Jourard, in proposing a remedy to this general societal hunger, says that there is a need for persons to become "transparent" in their transactions and events in everyday life. Otherwise, we live in a society of inauthenticity. He says that the remedy is to be found in mutual self-disclosure and in not continuing to live the life of just playing games with one another. He points out that the " 'Normal' self-alienated man, however, often ignores his 'tilt' signals—anxiety, guilt, boredom, pain, or frustration—and continues actions aimed at wealth, power, or normality until his body 'shrieks' loudly enough to be heard. The meaning of sickness is protest. . . . But, a change in direction could be termed growth, and it is in disclosing my real self that I finally get in a position to grow." [5]

Jourard's feeling was that what makes people "sick" or hungry, is found in the events and relationships of society: "Events, relationships, or transactions which give a person a sense of identity, or worth, of hope and of purpose in existence are 'inspiriting,' while those that make a person feel unimportant, worthless, hopeless, low in self-esteem, isolated and frustrated, and those that make him feel that existence is absurd and meaningless are 'dispiriting.' " [6] Thus, "wellness appears to ensue from such events as having one's individuality respected and acknowledged—hence the often beneficial effects of simple, nondirective counseling; i.e., of being listened to with understanding and of being touched. Being heard and touched by another who 'cares' seems to reinforce identity, mobilize spirit, and promote self-healing." [7]

Jourard's feeling is that the kind of society that we have created is one that is a "sick-making society." Therefore, the remedy is to have places and events where relationships are "reinvented," where human personality is affirmed; a total renewal of persons and the society around it. This is done through persons becoming "authentic beings" through self-disclosure of themselves.

Authentic being means being oneself, honestly, in one's relations with his fellows. It means taking the first step at dropping pretense, defenses, and duplicity. It means an end to 'playing it cool,' an end to using one's behavior as a gambit designed to disarm the other fellow, to get him to reveal himself *before* you disclose yourself to him. [8]

Evidences of a Spiritual Hunger

Over the past five or six years I've heard persons in churches describe hunger in many of the same terms as described above. I've had persons come up to me and start talking about their Christian experiences and before long I knew exactly what was being said for I've heard the same words, the same disillusionment, many times before. Or, often it's in a small sharing group somewhere in a church, and we've reached that stage where honesty and trust have become the climate that has bound us together in a new depth of fellowship, and persons will begin to share what they wished would happen in the life of their church or something that seemed to be missing from their own personal Christian experience.

The words go something like this: "I really would like to see something more 'relevant' going on in my church, or my life, than just attending meetings." "I sure am fed up with things as they are." "I wish I could be more authentic." "I feel like we are playing a game most of the time in Christianity." "I wish people really were more caring and concerned for one another." "The only thing I ever see us involved in is paving the parking lot, putting cushions on the pews, and buying a new organ." "When are we going to get around to working with the poor, the oppressed, the needy?" "I don't think we would know servanthood if it came down the aisle on Sunday morning and tried to join the church." "When are church and denominational leadership going to recognize that lay people make it possible for churches and the denomination to build all those things that are asked for in bigger budgets each year, and start letting us have a voice in the decision making process?" "The first thing I would do to change my church is to take the pews out so people wouldn't have to look at the back of each other's heads and would start seeing each other in the worship services again." "Everytime I try to propose something, the only answer I get is 'Don't rock the boat.' " "I want to see a more spiritual emphasis placed on what we do." "I am so hungry for a deeper spiritual walk with the Lord, but I don't know where to begin."

I could go on with other similar comments about the need for celebration in our lives, a rediscovery of the devotional life, knowing the joy of ministry through our daily work, and a willingness for God's people to be both vulnerable (free to fail) and affirming of others. What all of these expressions point to is a deep hunger within God's people for a deeper walk with him and other Christians. I believe that this is a hunger that has been produced by the work of the Holy Spirit as he calls us to new and deeper levels of obedience to the call of Christ to "Come, follow me."

Its difficult to ascribe to certain specific causes the reasons for the spiritual hunger that seems to be most evident among God's people. But, I believe the discussion of a basic hunger in society may provide clues. For one thing, these same feelings of men in society, which have been described above, have also invaded the life of churches. It should not be expected that the church could escape being affected by what happens to the lives of church members as they live out their work existence five and six days a week. It would be an oversimplification on my part, however, to say that these are the only things that have caused the loneliness, depersonalization, and alienation among persons, both in society and in churches. All I have tried to indicate is that some of those areas that have caused a hunger among persons in their daily living are also present in the life of most Christians. And, these people are looking to the church for some hope and for some answers to these and other questions about the changes that are happening all around them.

For the most part, as indicated by questions I have heard over the past several years of working with people in the areas of personal spiritual renewal and local church renewal, persons are not finding the answers in much of the normal activities of church groups of which they are part. They are finding, however, in lay weekends, retreats, and renewal conferences some signs of new hope. For most of them small groups have begun to provide new answers to the "hollow man," "the modular person," and the rootless "nation of strangers." But, why has the small group experience seemingly provided a partial answer to some deep basic longings of churches and Christians today?

Keith Miller, in his book, *The Becomers*, seeks to answer this question by utilizing Abraham Maslow's hierarchy of needs. This concept was developed by this American psychologist several years ago to show how different needs motivate people at different stages of their life. For instance a person who was still concerned about providing just enough money to keep body and soul together (safety needs) would not view life, including his church and Christian experience, in the same way as a person whose primary concern was for self-expression. This latter person would be at that point in life where he had an adequate income, a good home in the suburbs, and good schools for his children (self-actualization needs take over). The Christian experience, and consequently the church experience, for the person still concerned about safety needs might be a situation in which "eternal security" is the dominant theme of the preaching and the person's response to the gospel. In the case of the second person, it might not express itself in terms of a need for security, for in a sense that has already been met, but in a need for "realizing one's highest potential, for mature relationships with others, for religious and artistic expression, and for feelings of growth." [9]

Miller goes on to say that he believes that most denominations have within them "pockets of people" in many of the seven stages of need levels (not higher or lower stages though!), though different churches tend to speak to one particular "need level." Also, in many churches today there are persons who have grown up under one particular Christian teaching aimed at one need level, and they have found "upon growing up and learning the church's basic stance, that it has little to say to their own dominant needs." [10]

I believe that this has happened on a wider scale than most of us have believed in the past. In an alienated, depersonalized, lonely world, the need to belong; to be affirmed and to be cared for; the need for self-respect, approval and self-worth; the need to be involved in something that has relevance where I can fulfill my highest potential for growth and involvement; and the need to know and understand have taken over as that which dominates the primary motivation of many people who are looking for answers to some of those questions I have been hearing for the past few years.

Though Miller may have given us a general "need theory" for explaining the hunger that exists among churches and Christians today, I believe basically the search that is going on among Christians is part of a "journey into a new life-style" of deeper relationships with Christ in his call to "come, follow me." The two words that best express that hunger for me seem to be "disillusionment" and "disparity."

There seems to be a general disillusionment with either the Christian pilgrimage as I am presently experiencing it, or with the church as a place of fellowship and mission. I do not believe, as many, who have faulted those who were critical of the church, or have expressed dissatisfaction with their Christian experience, that this will "damage the church" or that "analysis leads to paralysis." I feel that the Reformation principle of the "church always being renewed," not one reformation is enough, is the better guide to follow.

If the Christian walk is a commitment of faith, then we too must be willing to be "wandering pilgrims" led constantly to deeper and deeper levels of faith and practice, not satisfied with where Christ has led today or where he led yesterday. The old story of the missionary who gave a sundial to the natives of a primitive tribe so they could order their lives only to come back some weeks later and find that they had built a hut over it and were worshiping it may be illustrative of where many who resist the pilgrimage of a faith-walk of the church and Christians are today. We have built our shrines over God's past experiences in our lives and have been unwilling to open to the possibility that he has any new and good gifts to bestow on us today and again tomorrow.

I believe that God's call to discipleship is a call to constant abandonment of the watering holes of yesterday to go on to explore new wells of commitment and discipleship. As someone has said, "It is a call to holy abandonment." Thus, disillusionment with the present and awareness of disparity between the scriptural demands of discipleship and the reality of present practice in personal Christian living and in the corporate life of the church may be a spiritual ministry of the Holy Spirit. I believe that the "Spirit of Truth" (John 14:17) does not leave us desolate forever, but leads us onward into new and deeper understandings of the Christian call to discipleship which "comfort" our dispair. Finally, that moment comes, again, when, just as we've got our Christian experience, and the corporate life of the Christian community "all tied up neat and nicely," the Holy Spirit comes along, and with his ministry of "holy discomfort," nudges us once more by saying to us, with whispers and hints of new gifts and new dimensions yet to be explored, that we've stayed here at this comfort station long enough.

It's time to push on again deeper and deeper into the pilgrimage of discipleship. So, for me, disillusionment and the growing awareness of the disparity between what is and what should be, should be welcomed by every pastor, church leader, and Christian as a ministry of the Holy Spirit, whom Jesus left to instruct us in Christian discipleship. Those who speak of pointing out weaknesses and failures as "rocking the boat" may be resisting the Spirit's work of holy discomfort.

Conclusion

A hunger, God's work of holy discomfort, is found in many Christians and churches today. It is both personal and corporate in its scope. But, basically renewal must begin with the hunger of persons. The hunger is recognizable as loneliness, hollowness, a search for authenticity, a need to know my real self, a need to establish meaningful relationships of a caring nature, and many other descriptive words.

This is a hunger to which the church and Christians can speak a word in power because of the Holy Spirit's gift of fellowship in a caring community. But, it is a gift that too many churches and Christians no longer know about. There is a need today for what Bruce Larson calls a "relational theology," which would, he says, "bring about an understanding of the underlying principles in life by which God heals, reconciles, loves, and makes us lovers of one another by His grace." [11] Keith Miller says the church has the "key" to the lonely cell of most persons by being personal. [12]

Henri Nouwen says that the church's answer to the hunger is first to recognize the wounds of this hunger in ourselves and then become "wounded healers" of others who also bear this same wound. Ours is a ministry to the hungry, lonely people around us, but ours is not a ministry of those whose "primary task is to take away pain. Rather . . . [ours is to] deepen the pain to a level where it can be shared. When someone comes with his loneliness . . . he can only expect that his loneliness will be understood and felt, so that he no longer has to run away from it but can accept it as an expression of his basic human condition." [13]

NOTES

1. Charles A. Reich, *The Greening of America* (New York: Random House, 1970), pp. 141-70, passim.

2. Alvin Toffler, *Future Shock* (New York: Random House, 1970), pp. 86-111, passim.

3. Vance Packard, *A Nation of Strangers* (New York: David McKay Co., 1972), pp. 2-4.

4. William Glasser, *The Identity Society* (New York: Harper & Row, 1972), pp. 8-9.

5. Sidney M. Jourard, *The Transparent Self* (New York: Van Nostrand Reinhold Co., 1971), pp. 27-32, passim.

6. *Ibid.*, p. 76.

7. *Ibid.*, p. 87.

8. *Ibid.*, p. 133.

9. Keith Miller, *The Becomers* (Waco: Word Books, 1973), pp. 89-109, passim.

10. *Ibid.*

11. Bruce Larson, *No Longer Strangers* (Waco: Word Books, 1971), pp. 17-26.

12. Miller, *op. cit.*, pp. 34 ff.

13. Henri J. M. Nouwen, *The Wounded Healer* (New York: Doubleday, 1972), p. 94.

3 Small Groups in the Church— Feeding Hungry People

The diagnosis has been made that something serious is ailing within Christianity, and that there is a basic hunger among God's people. Throughout the history of the church small groups have played a significant role in meeting the spiritual problems which Christians have faced. Thomas Oden in his book *The Intensive Group Experience* has pointed out the use of small groups by Christian leaders during times of church renewal in past centuries.

In our time, a new small group movement was begun in the 1940's by a group of social psychologists. Among them were men like Jacob Moreno and Kurt Lewin. Their work, along with other men like Carl Rogers, Fritz Perls, Abraham Maslow, Eric Berne, and William Schutz plowed new ground in the area of the psychology of how people relate to each other. What emerged from their studies during the following decades came out under such headings as group dynamics, small groups, encounter groups, growth groups, and training groups. Along the way in their research there also emerged new understandings about the potential for human growth as these same researchers became aware of what kept people from being free to become what they could become if their fullest potentials were realized. They discovered that social pressure not only caused people to conform, and thus distorted God-given potential, but at the same time could become the means by which potential could be tapped and released again. This has given rise to a whole new area of psychological studies which has been given the name "third force psychology" to distinguish it from the psychoanalytical approaches of Sigmund Freud and the behavoristic approaches of men like B. F. Skinner.

Small groups began to be used in industry meetings, in educational circles, and by the late fifties in the churches. I have tried to find an explanation for the literal explosion of small groups in various settings around the nation, and the most reasonable answer that seems to emerge over and over again is found in the description of much of the depersonalization, loneliness, and alienation felt by many persons as described in the preceding chapter. These people not only live a depersonalized, lonely, meaningless existence much of the time, but their rootlessness, because of high mobility along with the necessity of being very selective about which friends with whom to establish deep relationships, has left most people, even church people, with only superficial relationships. For many, this is no longer a satisfying way of life.

Also, along the way persons have lost the knowledge, maybe one that was inherent in rural society, of how to "get to know one another." The small group, with its techniques of building interpersonal relationships, seems to be reeducating a generation who hunger for authentic relationships within a caring, sharing community. It is providing a place where answers to deep questions of meaning and purpose in a society, where older values no longer seem to fit or hold up, can be explored. In the language of sociology, at one time we lived in "extended family" settings with aunts, uncles, cousins, and grandparents who could give more than one view-point to a problem. Today, most of us live in "one-generational" family settings: just me, my wife, and children. This has created a need for an "intergenerational" approach to life which can happen in small groups where persons from various backgrounds and ages get together to share in authentic relationships and share their deepest concerns.

Thus, the small groups seems to be a means for mobile, middle-class Americans, who live in suburbs away from their immediate families, working in offices where they are one cog in a great business enterprise, and feeling lonely, alienated, depersonalized, and helpless to voice any changes in the system, to recover some dimension of self-worth. Even churches, which have tended to have larger and larger organizations, unknowingly have perpetuated these same kinds of feelings in their members until a person resigns himself to: "That's the way all of life is; you can't change it." Or members resist, resign, and drop out.

Small Groups in the Church

Small groups, then, seem to have come along at the right time to offer an alternative expression of church for many persons looking for new depth in their own lives. At first small groups were used by the church in educational settings to brainstorm around some content area that had been presented by a teacher in a Sunday School class, or to get feedback from an idea that had been presented in a larger group presentation. In other words, the first use of small groups was as *an adjunct to the other educational approaches then being used.*

A second use of the small group was *in helping committees and boards of the church become sensitive to interpersonal relationships* so "they could get their job done more efficiently." This adaptation of small groups came directly from the business world where small groups and sensitivity sessions were being used to make management more efficient.

Small sharing groups also began to emerge spontaneously around the country in homes and churches to study the Bible, to pray, and to share what God was doing in their lives. One of the best adaptations of the small group has been in the *Lay Witness Missions in churches over the past few years.* In these Friday night to Sunday morning meetings, lay teams, who have paid their own way to come to a local church from many places, spend an entire weekend with other lay people telling them the ways in which God was at work in their lives. Part of what happened was done in small groups during the weekend, which has exposed many thousands of persons in churches to the use of sharing groups in the church.

Also, many places where I go I have groups of pastors meeting together to share with one another, not like the formal Monday morning pastor's conference, but in small groups sometimes called nothing more than the "strugglers group." But, in those small groups of pastors and other vocational church ministers, there has come support for their ministry and some meaning to the puzzling demands of the pastor's role in the church today.

What then are small groups? Part of the answer can be found in looking at the nature and purpose of small groups in the church. Robert Leslie had indicated certain features which, he feels, are present in all small groups in the church:

They are relatively small, ranging from eight to eighteen members. They meet as a self-conscious unit over a long enough period of time to develop a fairly intense sense of groupness, usually fifteen to twenty hours minimum. They meet in a relatively unstructured, agendaless way with a goal of greater awareness of self in relationship to others. Often some content is introduced, but the subject matter develops naturally rather than being formally introduced. The role of the leader is characteristically more of a catalyst than it is that of an authority. He strives to create a climate conducive to growth rather than to become the answer man. The focus is more on feeling than it is on rational thought, although a good deal of cognitive learning actually takes place.[1]

John Casteel, on the other hand, has described small groups in the church in this way:

A personal group is a small number of persons, meeting face to face regularly for the purposes of the study of the Bible and of the Christian faith; for prayer; for the exchange of experiences, needs, and insights; and for taking thought as to how they can best fulfill their calling as Christians to love and serve God and other people.[2]

Thus, essential elements for small groups in a church seem to be: (1) a *definable membership* meeting on a regular basis in a face to face relationship—this means that persons cannot just drop in to "sample" whenever they feel like it, nor can persons visit from time to time without making a commitment to the other group members; (2) there develops a sense of *common identity* which says that the group achieves a group consciousness of itself; (3) at the same time the group develops a *common purpose* which holds it on a definite direction; (4) a binding sense of *interdependence* emerges which can be labeled as "community" for all are participants (there are no spectators) and such elements as acceptance, mutual accountability, trust, honesty, risking, caring, sharing, and commitment are present; and (5) there grows out of the group a *self-administered discipline* (some would call this the "group contract," but it usually involves those things that hold persons accountable for personal growth and mutual support).

Small Groups As an Expression of an Emerging Life-style

A sixth characteristic of the small group, though it may be

found in an implied way in the above five elements, is found in a _commitment to personal growth and maturity_. It is described in various ways as "being in process," or "under construction," or as Keith Miller has so beautifully written of it, "becoming." Whatever the phrase to describe it, even in the phrase of the humanistic psychologist, Abraham Maslow, "self-actualization," it means giving up old patterns of immaturity and self-defeating behavior and beginning a movement towards maturity and health. This is what Jesus described as "life more abundantly."

This kind of stance of those in small groups is really a movement towards a new Christian life-style in the church as persons adopt new ways of being and living, Bruce Larson has described this new life-style with the two words "affirmation" and "vulnerability." He says that this new style of Christian living is one "that will allow people to discover their worth, their strengths, and their uniqueness, and to communicate how much God intends to do with them and for them." [3] In another book Larson has described it as "living on the growing edge." He said it is living at that point of openness in our lives where God threatens us most and where we feel least comfortable. [4]

For those on pilgrimage towards personal growth in small groups, God's "holy discomfort" takes over again and again—many times, not just once or twice—as new dimensions of inauthentic and false selves are faced and laid aside. Thomas Merton called this constant encountering of inauthenticity, "holy dread." [5] It is the constant recognition at deeper levels of our being of false identities which have to be faced in order for authentic life to emerge in Christ.

Thus, the word "freedom" has described one of the dimensions of the life-style of those who have participated in small groups. It has come to mean a movement from bondage to becoming free enough to be the person God created them to be. They have become free from acting out of roles, from behind masks, because they thought persons would not accept them as they were. In fact, as long as we act out of roles or continue to wear the masks, "there is no possibility of human and personal growth." It is for this reason that the small group and personal Christian growth are intertwined.

The small group also has become for many what the larger congregation simply could not do because of its size and the very way its existence is structured. It has become the the the "small church within the church." It is in the small group that God seems best able to give his gift of *koinonia*—fellowship. The small group becomes, then, the living embodiment of community. Reuel Howe has said, the essence of community is dialogue:

How does the church or any group of people become a community? And the answer is simple: it becomes a community when as persons, the members enter into dialogue with one another and assume responsibility for their common life. Without this dialogue individuals and society are abstractions. It is through dialogue that man accomplishes the miracle of personhood and community.[6]

The small group thus becomes the place where, as I experience community in acceptance and dialogue, I attempt my first small steps of growth. It involves risk, but it leads to that point where I can become free enough to become the Christ-intended person for which I have the God-given potential; and to become free enough to begin to be led by the nudgings of the Holy Spirit into deeper and deeper dimensions of personal Christian living and their expression in the community of faith, the church. It is a movement towards true Christian authenticity.

I see three areas in which small groups will provide growth in a new life-style in the church today: (1) growth in *koinonia*—fellowship; (2) growth in personal Christian depth; and (3) growth in mission (both in ministry and witness). These areas of growth will help provide new answers, through the rebuilding of small sharing and caring units within the life of the church, to institutional deadness; to the depersonalization that is a part of society and the church; and to the releasing of a new power of the church in ministry and witness.

In this way, church members—who no longer know each other so that fellowship has become, not a gift that God gives his people to enrich their style of living together as the body of Christ, but a program done once a month, or the name of the place where we eat (fellowship hall)—can begin to be experienced again in the richness of what Bonhoeffer called "life together."

Not only will small groups in the church assist persons in a deepening of their personal relationships with others, but they can become the means for restoring a sense of mission to the church. Mission is the vocation and the calling of all who follow Christ. Ministry and witness belong primarily to the laity, and the clergy exist to equip and enable God's people for their mission in the world (Eph. 4:11-12). The Holy Spirit gives his gifts on behalf of the church to God's people for their witness and ministry, and the role of church education is for the nurture and equipment of God's people for their mission in the world.

Thus, the most lasting and permanent contribution of the small group movement to the life of the church may be found in two types of small groups in the church; the small sharing group and the small mission group. In these two expressions of small groups the life of the church is being called to take seriously two dimensions basic to its biblical rootage: the priesthood of the laity; and the need to build "indepth community" into the life of the church.

If the nature of the church is basically "fellowship" (*koinonia*) and the purpose of the church exists for joining God in his reconciling work of healing the world's brokenness, then what better way to do this than through small groups which come together for sharing and mission? Thus, small groups are a call to feeding lonely, hungry people so that God's people may experience new dimensions of fellowship, and to join God in mission to society's brokenness. This is a call to a life-style change in persons and churches.

Sharing Groups and Mission Groups

Sharing groups and mission groups, in the language of sociological and psychological literature would fit most nearly into the two basic classifications of small groups. Groups tend to be either for the purpose of personal growth or for the performance of a task. Though groups tend to be one or the other of these two types, the ideal would be to have a combination of personal growth as well as a concern with a task. But this would mean that a small group would have to move from a one-dimensional characteristic to a multidimensional one.

Sharing groups tend to be personal growth groups, though there is an introduction to some tasks; and in this sense, they tend to be one-dimensional groups which have a very narrow focus of concern. This explains the variety of names given to sharing groups for they tend to focus around a particular concern, either to study the Bible, to meet for prayer, or to enrich marriage relationships.

Sharing groups find their basic purpose in the facillitation of sharing between persons at a deeper level than normally takes place in most conversation and communication in the life of the church.

Someone has described three levels of communication which happen between persons: the first might be called "mouth to mouth" communication, which is the most normal type, and is expressed in the phrases, "How are you?" "how are you getting along?" or "How are you doing?" The person asking does not really care for you to stop him and describe all of the latest symptoms that are bothering you. These are phrases that we use, such as, "Good to see you," which keep communications open, but at a superficial level with the numerous people with whom we come into contact every day, even in a church with five hundred members or more. You simply cannot know each and every one in much more than this level of word communication, which is an acknowledgement of existence.

A second level of communication might be called "head-to-head" or that which we do in the communication of ideas from one person to another. This is also an important way for interpersonal communication, but it involves persons only at one level of their existence, the ideas and concepts that are accepted or rejected in our attempt to influence the way a person structures the information that flows into his life each day.

Each of us has a "filter" or a structure through which, or onto which, we understand and accept, or reject new or old information. All around us at every moment in our lives there are transmitters of information to us. Some of the transmitters are persons and other things. But, we are constantly being bombarded with stimuli that we filter in, or filter out, according to some predisposition that we have. Those who communicate ideas to us are constantly seeking to get through that filter in order for their ideas to be heard and possibly accepted by us. Our filter, again, helps us to both tune in, and to tune out, the overabundance of idea communications that come to us from radios, televisions, advertisements, politicians, and many other sources.

A third level of communication may be called "heart-to-heart" which implies a communication that is personal versus superficial, and which involves the total person including his deepest feelings. It is at this level of communication that we share ourselves at our most honest and open dimensions. And, this is a sharing that is done only with a small number of people, for it is the most intimate kind of sharing. It is a kind of sharing that is expressed in the New Testament word *koinonia* or fellowship.

Because sharing at this deeper level of communication is basic to sharing groups in the church, most small groups which exist in churches today (excluding existing educational organizations which tend to be task groups) are in some way or form basically sharing groups. They may have come together around some particular title, which expresses part of their purpose, but basically they are sharing groups for the level of communication, if it does not remain superficial, is that of interpersonal "heart-to-heart" sharing.

"Mouth-to-mouth" and "head-to-head" communication do not tend to reach the level of deep interpersonal sharing, which we have already described as the basic hunger of society and many church members today. They have their place and purpose, but they cannot supply what is needed in building deep caring and sharing relationships in the life of the church. The superficial greeting, though it is necessary, and the communicating of ideas, though essential to the functioning of organizations, are not sufficient for the total well-being of persons or churches. A church cannot exist at a sufficiently deep enough level to be a healer of the wounds of society if it does not also build those communication units, called sharing groups, within the church where God can give his gift of fellowship. Fellowship cannot be given by just talking about it, nor simply by planning a "fellowship" after the evening service where "mouth-to-mouth" communications take place.

Thus, Leslie has said of sharing groups, "the focus is more on feeling than it is on rational thought, although a good deal of cognitive learning actually takes place." [7] Indicating other characteristics of a sharing group he continues: "This type of group is obviously different from the more usual study group in which the focus is on a body of material. Here the focus is on the persons present and on the feelings that they are experiencing. Here is a group structure in which sharing is not only emphasized, but one in which sharing is the chief characteristic." [8] Finally, Leslie says that this kind of group "has as its primary concern the recognizing and the meeting of the individual need of its members. The . . . group aims at communication in its freest, most uninhibited, most personal sense." [9]

Mission groups, as they are discussed in this book, may seem to be task-oriented, but because of their commitment to many areas of personal and corporate Christianity, they are really multidimensional groups. The dimensions of building indepth, disciplined community; self-awareness; discovery of personal gifts for mission; development of the quiet center of the devotional life; systematic Bible study; sharing of material resources; and involvement in mission, are *all* handled *at the same time* in the life of the mission group. Though the tendency, by the very name of mission group, is to make them only task-oriented, and thus only one-dimensional, mission groups as they are presented here seek to hold the two dimensions of personal growth (the journey inward) and the task-centeredness (journey outward) in creative tension. The sharing group does not try to do this, but attempts only to *introduce* a person to these dimensions of the Christian pilgrimage in a one-dimensional setting and in a climate of acceptance, honesty, and exploration. More will be said about this second basic type of small group in the church in a later chapter.

NOTES

1. Robert C. Leslie, *Sharing Groups in the Church* (Nashville: Abingdon Press, 1971), p. 25.

2. John L. Casteel, *Spiritual Renewal Through Personal Groups* (New York: Association Press, 1957), p. 19.

3. Larson, *op. cit.,* p. 53.

4. Larson, *Living on the Growing Edge* (Grand Rapids: Zondervan Publishing House, 1968), p. 19.

5. Thomas Merton, *Contemplative Prayer* (New York: Imge Books, 1969), pp. 97 ff.

6. Reuel L. Howe, *The Miracle of Dialogue* (New York: The Seabury Press, 1963), p. 5.

7. Leslie, *op. cit.*, p. 25.

8. *Ibid.*, p. 47.

9. *Ibid.*, p. 117.

4 Sharing Groups—Growth in Koinonia

Sharing groups in the church serve as a preparatory structure for an exploration of growth primarily in two areas of personal and corporate Christian life: growth in *koinonia* and growth in personal depth. However, when a person enters a sharing group, his commitment should be based on his acceptance by the group, and *not* on his commitment that he has to change. He is accepted into the group where, in a climate of openness, honesty, and exploration, he is not only affirmed, but he becomes painfully aware of his self-defeating behavior and the fact that he is, in spite of all the attempts to be a good churchman, an unprofitable servant. As Lyman Coleman has said: "You 'enable' each other by pointing out the positive traits you have observed. Then, in the atmosphere of warmth and affirmation, each person shares the thing that he would like to change about himself."

Since, participation in sharing groups is voluntary, persons should be invited to participate in them, and not promoted along the usual lines of "everyone has to be in one." Leslie warns:

In any church group there will be some who will not change. It is not that they do not want to, or that they have no need to, but the patterns of behavior are so firmly fixed and the defenses so strongly built that any change would call for a major re-working of patterns of life. Some ego defenses need to be retained, and it is not the purpose of the church sharing group to tear them down. An acceptance of a person the way he is, is the first step toward making the possibility for change real.[1]

Thus, we must be aware of the "brittle" persons who, in their rigid patterns, are threatened by the lack of usual structure, which is found in a loosely structured sharing group, and never insist that they attend a sharing group, or once in sharing group, compel them to share. This does nothing more than create more resistance to the kind of free sharing of feelings which is the purpose of a sharing group.

"A large part of the uniqueness of the sharing group lies in the experience of communicating freely, without defensiveness, in as personal and emotional a manner as one desires. Ideally, the sharing group is one in which it is possible to be perfectly honest about emotions present as they are recognized in the self and shared with others." [2] Therefore, a sharing group should not compel persons to join, nor to trap them into sharing beyond that which they are willing to share at that moment. Those, who model risk, freedom, and an ability to operate out of gift, call out the freedom and gifts of others. And, it does no good to push butterflies out of cocoons until they are ready without damaging them, maybe permanently.

Therefore, the sharing group serves the purpose in the church of being a place to "try on," "to taste," "to explore" the deeper dimensions of discipleship. This is especially essential in the life of the church today where there exists a hunger generated both by the societal circumstances around modern man and a desire on the part of many Christians to move beyond existing church structures into new and exciting areas of Christian living.

Dimensions of Christian experience will begin to emerge in elementary and undeveloped forms in sharing groups which serve the purpose of introducing, in a preparatory fashion, persons to certain essential elements of a journey into a deeper Christian life-style: disciplined Christian community; self-awareness; discovery of personal gifts for mission; development of the quiet center of the devotional life where one can encounter God at a deeper level; systematic Bible study; and awareness of God's mission of reconciliation. All of these are encountered in a rudimentary form in the first two areas of growth through groups. Serious involvement in a structure for indepth study and a mission group follow.

Since growth in *koinonia* and personal Christian growth are prerequisites for growth in mission, let's examine the first of these two areas of growth, growth in *koinonia*.

Growth in Koinonia

Koinonia, or as translated in English, "fellowship," is what the church is all about according to the Scriptures, but not according to practice in much of church life today. As church structures have been built over the last two decades, they have tended to take the "auditorium" format which was built for performances, for performers and spectators, and that is exactly what many church services have become, including all of the theatrical gimmicks of modern times, such as the dimming of lights and the spotlight on the performer.

Church structures have always reflected in some way the basic understandings of the times as to what the nature and the purpose of the church was all about. Thus, it was in the fourth century, when Constantine wanted to build four churches in the city of Rome to honor Peter, Paul, John, and Mary he choose the structural form of the basilica, which had originally been built to house the Roman Government.[3] Thus, the use of the imposing structure of the basilica in a real sense was a stating of the alignment of the ruling power of the Roman government with Christianity. Other illustrations throughout the history of the Christian church could be given in which architecture expressed something about the basic understanding of the church and its life.

The tragedy with the auditorium of today's church building is that as the size of the churches themselves have grown, the size of the auditorium has also grown—longer. This has made church life, along with the complexity of their many activities, very impersonal, and thus there is a perpetuation of exactly the problems of society where church members live out the other six days of their lives.

Yet, the church, by its very prupose is *koinonia*. Emil Brunner, twenty years ago, pointed out that the true essence of the church is *koinonia:*

The Ekklesia is never conceived of as institutional; but exclusively as a fellowship of persons, as the common life based in fellowship with Jesus Christ as a fellowship of the Spirit (*koinonia pneumatos*) and a fellowship of Christ (*koinonia Christou*). To be in Christ through faith and to be in this fellowship are one and the same thing.[4]

Brunner went on to condemn the church for its misunderstanding of this basic essence to its life when he said, "that fellowship is the theme of the Gospel of Jesus and the Apostles, not only is missing from the churches, but quite often is simply not desired there." [5]

Perhaps the best word with which to communicate the word "fellowship" today, and the word that is rich with meaning from the study of the dynamics of small groups, is the word "community." Elizabeth O'Connor has said that community is an "engagement with others in depth." [6] As such, it is not built on our usual criteria of fellowship defined in such words as "togetherness," "groupness," or "getting together." These are all terms that assume only fellowship on the basis of human affinity, human association, or social relationships. It is possible, even in a small group, to have twelve "warm bodies" in a room, and unless there is some type of interaction among the persons present, there is no community. But, let one person begin to share deeply and personally out of his own struggles with the Christian pilgrimage, and God's gift of community begins.

Thus, community, or fellowship, consists in a sense of oneness, life lived with each other at sufficient depth for each person to be heard, accepted, in openness, honesty, in the process of discovering the real self (including his gifts for ministry), authenticity (stopping the playing of games and the wearing of masks), and in the process of becoming whole (the root meaning of salvation). At the same time the other persons in the group have to be really "present" to each person in the group as they share and not just nodding the head, but being far away in thought.

Douglas Steere wrote a powerful little pamphlet, which I came across several years ago, called "On Being Present Where You Are." In it he described what I think are the dimensions of community, this koinonia, which I am describing. Most of the time, we simply are not present to each other. That is what makes the difference between the greetings of "hello;" the exchanges of ideas; and the communications which I have called "heart-to-heart." And, this is the quality we must grow in if we are to grow in *koinonia*. We have to be really present to each other, and not have your eyes become glassy and glazed over as we drift off into our phantasy land; or plan our next comment which will outdo what you are trying to say; or plan the next question which will destroy what you are trying to communicate.

Steere says that being present to one another is a posture of readiness to respect and to stand in wonder and openness before the mysterious life and influence of the other. It means, to be sure, a power to influence, to penetrate, to engage with the other; but it means equally a willingness to be vulnerable enough to be influenced by, to be penetrated by, and even to be changed by the experience.[7]

He goes on to describe additional dimensions of "being present" to another person as he says:

Each is willing to drop, or at least to lower, the projected image and to feel an increasing sense of responsibility that the other should fulfill the mysterious destiny that God has hidden within him whether this shatters the image or not. Each counts it an infinite blessing to be able to live in the presence of the other and to be forever surprised by the joy of seeing the other grow from the deepest inner vision that is hidden in him.[8]

But, the cost of this kind of presence is demanding. "For really to be present to another, to be a true friend, means to be forever on call, forever open, forever willing to be involved in the friend's troubles as well as his joys."[9] It is this cost and responsible commitment to it that, I believe, keeps us from being a community in most of our church groups today. Yet, in sharing and mission groups, if there is real *koinonia* to emerge and grow, we must make this kind of costly commitment to each other—to be really present to each other in the sharing group, and not just to perpetuate the "togetherness" of past such groupings.

Gordon Cosby has said of this commitment to be a community:

It says to a specific group of people that I am willing to be with you. I am willing to belong to you, I am willing to be the people of God with you. This is never a tentative commitment that I can withdraw from. It is a commitment to a group of miserable, faltering sinners who make with me a covenant to live in depth until we see in each other the mystery of Christ Himself and until in these relationships we come to know ourselves as belonging to the Body of Christ.[10]

Being in community not only means being present to each other, but it also means giving up the illusion of the *ideal* community, or the wish-dream that each of us entertains about what fellowship "ought to be like." It means being willing to let go of our ideals and wishes and allow God to create within the group something new of his own. This means that community takes seriously both the corporateness of its identity (something which is very hard for us to give up in our individualistically oriented society and church life) and the divine origin of community. Being a corporate people means I must give up some part of myself in order for the group's identity to emerge, and this is a call to death which most of us avoid.

It also means that God is the creator of whatever community emerges as persons take seriously the corporateness of their common pilgrimage. Bonhoeffer said that the basis of any religious community "consists solely in what Christ has done to both of us." Most of us would readily agree to that, but it is in the cost of building on that reality that we begin to encounter the pain/joy tension of community. The first of these pains is giving up my idea of community, a letting go in order for God to take over the leadership of the group. Bonhoeffer said of this cost of community: "The man who fashions a visionary ideal of community, demands that it be realized by God, by others, and by himself. He enters the community of Christians with his demands, sets up his own law, and judges the brethren and God Himself accordingly." [11] Thus, a group must let go and let God realize the divine elements within the group.

But, also involved in a group knowing *koinonia* within its midst is the degree to which it will commit itself to openness, sharing, honesty, and a search for authentic dimensions of one's self. Bruce Larson said:

No one is more lonely than two Christians living together or working side by side and pretending to be better than they are. Some of the most astonishing miracles I have seen have occurred when Christians have stopped playing games and dared to appropriate the power that God has made available in Christ. Because of this power, they have dared to love each other enough to reveal those things about themselves that could be threatening or damaging.[12]

O'Connor also sums up this capacity for a group to be open, honest, and sharing at deep levels:

In this strange community where commitment is not tentative we become free to act and to speak. We can take risks that we could not take in other situations, which include the risk of getting in touch with our own unfelt feelings. We can afford to express negative reactions and move toward meeting, if we know our words do not cut us off. We can choose to express anger and therefore keep the sun from setting on it. We can take the risk of telling a brother what stands between us, if we know there will be another time when we are together, and that it does not depend on what does or does not happen in this moment.[13]

Though there is a temptation to withdraw at moments of crisis, we must never be tempted to make peace the price of community. Sometimes tension is the most productive element of a community as we are forced to deal with false selves and shallow understandings of the Christian pilgrimage. But, that which holds us together as we are in community is that which Christ has done in each of us and is in the process of constructing. Concerning their church, O'Connor also said: "It had been acts of confession that bound us together in community of caring and released a healing power that must be experienced again and again in the process of being made whole." [14]

This depth of community, however, depends on two dimensions of life together: acceptance and respect for a person's privacy. If there is enough acceptance in the sharing group of the individual; if they can be fully present to him; then they may share their real feelings, and "the church will recover again the grace of confession." But, there must be a willingness in a group for both what is shared to be held in confidence and for a person to feel free enough to not have to share; the right to have a "trapdoor" or to have some rooms that are not ready to be shared.

At first the account that we give of ourselves may be faltering and superficial, but it is movement toward seeing ourselves as we are, and taking the next step in the awakening process. We do not have to be where we are not, or force ourselves, or let others push us into giving accounts that we are not ready to give.

There will be no community unless we can learn to share our lives, but neither will there be any community where these does not exist a deep respect for privacy. One of the brighter discoveries of growing up is that one does not have to lie to keep his secret. There are questions addressed to us that we do not have to answer.[15]

But, when that moment comes when I can put into words what I am feeling, I can become free of another dimension in my life that keeps me from being an authentic person in community.

Community is also characterized by the discovery of my real self, to begin to like the "me" that God has created and to know my gifts for ministry. O'Connor says that church or community, is really a "gift-evoking community" [16] for "where God calls a person, he calls him into the fullness of his own potential." This means that the group affirms me as a person of worth; it calls out from within me gifts that I am not aware I have, or have been unwilling, as the servant who buried his one talent, to allow to be seen; and thus community becomes an affirmer of my capacity to also be an evoker of freedom and gifts in others. W. O. Thomason calls these people who are enabled to do this for each other "life-givers."

We can thank God that always among us are people, ~~life-givers~~, who have the capacity to see within us what we are and what we can be. How often has anyone talked for a moment, then minutes, or an hour about what you might become? Most of us can count on one hand the times in our life when this has happened. The life giver is one who has the capacity to see possibilities in persons when all others around see impossibilities. The life giver is one who can accept persons when others have already begun to reject the same person.[17]

Conclusion

Community, therefore, is a gift of God, but it is given through a group of people who come together to struggle and search for deeper meanings of *koinonia* than are currently being experienced in the lives of most Christians. Sharing groups and mission groups are places where the new dimensions of this gift that God has for his people are found. It is given sometimes in pain, but also in joy.

The hope, and the cost, of growth in *koinonia* is expressed by O'Connor in these two statements: "There will be no peace or healing in our day unless little islands of *koinonia* can spring up everywhere—islands where Christ is, and because He is we can learn to live a new way." [18] And, "We cannot begin to cope with what it means to build a world community unless we understand how difficult it is to be in community even with a small group of people, presumably called by their Lord to the same mission." [19]

These statements, I think, point to the necessity of sharing groups struggling with the dimensions of growth in *koinonia* for it is basic for the reestablishment of community within the large church institutions which we have built, and for ministering to the lonely, depersonalized, alienated persons within them and within society. We need only to be reminded of how the early church was described in one of the few passages in the New Testament that uses the word *koinonia*:

And they devoted themselves to the apostles' teaching and fellowship, to the breaking of bread and prayers. And fear came upon every soul; and many wonders and signs were done through the apostles. And all who believed were together and had all things in common; and they sold their possessions and goods and distributed them to all, as any had need. And day by day, attending the temple together and breaking bread in their homes, they partook of food with glad and generous hearts, praising God and having favor with all the people (Acts 2:42-47, RSV).

Dietrich Bonhoeffer, commenting on this passage, said:

When a community has such a source and goal it is a perfect communion of fellowship, in which even material goods fall into their appointed place. In freedom, joy and the power of the Holy Spirit a pattern of common life is produced where 'neither was there among them any that lacked,' where 'distribution was made unto each according as anyone had need,' where 'not one of them said that aught of the things which he possesed was his own.' In the everyday quality of these events we see a perfect picture of that evangelical liberty where there is no need of compulsion. They were indeed 'of one heart and soul.' This infant Church was a visible community which all the world could see.[20]

Thus, they, like sharing groups in the church, modeled *koinonia* for the hunger that was around them, and the Scriptures say there were "added to their number day by day." And a few verses later it says, after noting again the qualities of this community, that the apostles had "great power" in giving their testimony (Acts 4:32-35). Could it be that growth in *koinonia* would have this same effect in the lives of our churches today, if we were willing to pay the price of building and growing in *koinonia*—

numbers being added daily, and a new power being demonstrated in the life of the church which is available to us through the Holy Spirit? I believe that God is ready, if we are ready to receive, to give his gift of *koinonia* through sharing groups to the church and to the world.

NOTES

1. Leslie, *op. cit.*, p. 158.

2. *Ibid.*, p. 142.

3. James F. White, *Protestant Worship and Church Architecture* (New York: Oxford Press, 1964), pp. 55 ff. It is interesting to note White's comments concerning this major change in church buildings from "house churches" to the imposing style of the basilica: "An almost inevitable consequence was the loss of intimacy of the small Christian group. Increasingly the clergy performed the acts of worship with the laity becoming more and more passive" (p. 56). I wonder what future historians will say have been the consequences of the church building "boom" of the 1950's and 1960's on fellowship in the life of American Protestantism because of the construction of the long "halls of worship"?

4. Emil Brunner, *Dogmatics*, Vo. 3 (Philadelphia: The Westminster Press, 1962), p. 21.

5. Brunner, *The Misunderstanding of the Church* (Philadelphia: The Westminster Press, 1953), p. 51.

6. Elizabeth O'Conner, *Journey Inward, Journey Outward* (New York: Harper & Row, 1968), p. 24.

7. Douglas V. Steere, *"On Being Present Where You Are,"* (Wallingford, Penn.: Pendle Hill Pub., 1967), p. 9.

8. *Ibid.*, p. 11.

9. *Ibid.*, p. 15.

10. O'Connor, *op. cit.*, p. 24.

11. Dietrich Bonhoeffer, *Life Together* (London: SCM Press, 1954), p. 15-17.

12. Bruce Larson, *No Longer Strangers* (Waco: Word Books, 1971), p. 94.

13. O'Connor, *op. cit.*, p. 25.

14. O'Connor, *Search for Silence* (Waco: Word Books, 1972), p. 19.

15. *Ibid.*, p. 39

16. O'Connor, *Eighth Day of Creation* (Waco: Word Books, 1971), p. 8.

17. W. O. Thomason, *The Life Givers* (Nashville: Broadman Press, 1972), pp. 56-57.

18. O'Connor, *Call to Commitment* (New York: Harper & Row, 1963), pp. 40-41.

19. O'Connor, *Journey Inward, Journey Outward*, p. 8.

20. Bonhoeffer, *The Cost of Discipleship* (New York: The Macmillan Co., 1959), p. 285.

5 Sharing Groups—Growth in Personal Depth

Personal Christian growth and maturity, or as it may be called "spiritual formation," is the second concern of sharing groups as well as mission groups. Growth in personal depth simply means a deepening of the personal Christian life, and the two dimensions of it are growth in self-awareness and a deepening of a daily encounter with God through prayer, meditation, contemplation.

Someone once noted that human beings may not be perfectable, but they are improvable. This is the concern about growth experienced in small sharing groups, a direction that continues in greater depth in mission groups. Persons come to examine in depth the dimensions of their own personal Christian growth and maturity; their "journey inward." Paul has beautifully stated this as the goal of the Christian life in his letter to the church at Colossae: "You have put on a new self which will progress towards true knowledge the more it is renewed in the image of its creator." (Col. 3:10, *The Jerusalem Bible*).

Daily renewal as a goal of Christian growth could be stated by the term "Christian potential." This term seeks to open up new dimensions of an area normally known as Christian education in our churches.

Christian education, sometimes called church education or religious education, has defined itself over the years with various terms like nurture, moral education, indoctrination, affective education, cognitive education, and many others. In recent years there have come new terms like education for mission, value education, life-style education and education for engagement. But, what I think may be a more adequate goal for Christian education in its concern for Christian growth and maturity, is bound up in the phrase "free to achieve my Christian potential."

When I was growing up, Christian education was spoken of

in one of two kinds of categories, although I am sure there were many more. One of those educational categories was stated in terms of "do's" and "don't's." Growth and Christian maturity was supposedly measured in how many things you could move from the "don't column" into the "do column." Each person had his own private list of what you were not supposed to do, and what was expected of you. But, also, the church, in its Christian education program and in its preaching services, and just general church life, made you abundantly aware of what was expected in each of these two columns. Therefore, it was not too difficult to judge whether a person had achieved a certain degree of Christian maturity by the number of items he had been able to transfer from the don't category to the do category. These columns were almost memorized if not ingrained in the life of the church and the family. This kind of measurement even created controversies in the lives of churches as to what belonged in each column with much difference of opinion as values changed from rural to urban life-styles.

You can, I am sure name the "do's" and "don't's" that were in your background, and these served for many people as an easy quick reference as to where a person was in terms of his/her Christian maturity and growth. The only problem with this approach recently is that more and more of the items in each column have come to be challenged and some have been eliminated all together because of social pressure of their lack of integrity when placed alongside of the Christian demands of discipleship.

The other way of defining Christian maturity and growth when I was growing up was in terms of attendance and belonging to certain organizations and meetings in the life of the church. You were counted to be a "five-star" Christian if you were a member and attended regularly Sunday School, Training Union, a missionary organization, (later the church music program was added), Sunday morning and Sunday evening worship, mid-week prayer service, and any other special meetings of the church. We even gave gold stars to award persons for meeting these standards of Christian growth, which were primarily measured in terms of belonging, attendance, and the meeting of some standards of membership which were assigned a percentage point so that a weekly grade of spiritual maturity and growth could be achieved. It should be noted here that these standards of membership were in effect very close to the concept of the small group disciplines, but since they were never enforced, they became practically meaningless.

What we have done in burdening people with these percentage measurements of Christian growth and maturity, and in defining it primarily in terms of belonging and attendance is to render them powerless and drive people to ignore them all together. The proverbial story of the little old lady who said, "I would become a Southern Baptist, but I am not physically up to it," may be all too true.

Those were the understandings of Christian growth I grew up with, and I am sure the same definitions many continue to struggle with today. But, somewhere along the way I became disillusioned with those measurements and began to seek something more satisfying. At first my disillusionment took the form of criticism of what was, but I wasn't sure what should be in its place. Some persons were receptive and supportive of me during that time of struggle and search, and others critical and unsympathetic, which often made me more critical and angry. Since then, I have learned that disillusionment and a discovery of the disparity between what is and what the scriptural teachings indicate, is a ministry of the Holy Spirit in his ministry of holy discomfort. He pushes us on to deeper and deeper understandings of what Jesus has been calling us to be as His new people on mission.

Those of us, who in the decade of the 1960's were critical of the church and wrote and spoke about its points of inadequacy, failures, and shortcomings were speaking and writing out of our own despair and disillusionment. But, growth begins precisely in hunger; a hunger that says this way is no longer "good news" to me. Thomas Harris has written that three things are necessary for a person to want to change: (1) you must hurt sufficiently so that you want to change; (2) a slow type of despair sets in—boredom; or (3) you make a sudden discovery that you can change.[1]

Now, I didn't start out to change, to grow, that came later. Hunger was what drove me to grow, and Leslie points out one of the dangers of sharing groups is to announce at the very

beginning that you will *have to change* if you join "our group."
He says "if change is presented as a requirement for membership,
legitimate hostility can be expected. Much of the failure of church
groups has grown out of the fact that change seemed to be
demanded when no contract for making changes had been accepted." [2] He advises to allow people in sharing groups (this is
different from the process of mission groups) to participate at
whatever level they are interested in. (And, this is precisely what
makes a sharing group a preparatory structure. The same is true
of in-depth study structures where persons can join at whatever
level of interest or commitment they find themselves. However,
in mission groups, a new level of understanding and commitment
is required. This will be examined later.)

What has been my own personal experience, and I think that
which Leslie confirms in this comment, is that hunger must pre-
cede a desire to grow. He says that growth comes not by compulsion but by a combination of understanding acceptance and gentle
challenge. Thus, hunger is a spiritual ministry and those who have
crushed criticism and disillusionment, or simply tried to gloss them
over, have not been sensitive to this work of the Holy Spirit to
call God's people to even greater dimensions of Christian growth
and maturity.

Disillusionment, a hurting sufficiently, a drivenness to seek
something different is the beginning, and in my own search for
what Christian growth and maturity was all about, several
persons ministered to me in pointing the way, but it all seemed
to come together more recently in the words "Christian potential."
This is obviously a taking over of the words from am emerging
field of psychological studies which have been given the title
of "third force psychology." The men in this field of psychological
studies are the same ones mentioned previously as also being
responsible for the small group movement, and the interrela-
tionship between their studies of small groups and achieving
human potential is easily understood. They were persons looking
for ways in which to unlock the potential they saw in persons,
and at the same time saw the small group as the best means
for accomplishing that end.

Yet, the term human potential is probably best associated with

one man more than any other, Abraham Maslow. Frank Goble
in writing about this new thrust of psychological studies said that
Maslow was different from either Sigmund Freud, who majored
primarily on mental illnesses, or the behaviorists, like B. F. Skinner,
who tended to study averages of human behavior. To the Freudians
he said, "How can you understand mental illness until you understand mental health?" And the behaviorists he chided on
their study of what average people could do which tended
"to lead to the concept of the 'well-adjusted' person rather than
the well 'developed personality." [3]

I suppose it is in his disagreement with the behavioral psychologists that Maslow showed his greatest distinction, for he said
that what had happened all along as social scientists had studied
man in trying to understand him was to state what was the
"average," expected, or normal behavior, rather than what was
man's potential. Instead, Maslow found that one could learn a
great deal about man and his potential from the study of excep-
tionally healthy, mature people.

This person, who would serve as a model for "human potential,"
Maslow variously called as a self-actualized person or a person
who was on the "growing tip" of humanity, and one who could
indicate to the rest of humanity what *could be* in their lives.
Goble explains this understanding in these terms:

This approach was a rejection of the customary statistical approach
used in behavioral science which takes the average of the species. The
example he used was: if you wanted to know how fast a man could
run a mile or how to improve your ability to run a mile, you didn't
study the average runner, you studied the exceptional runner, those
at the growing tip. Only those individuals will give you an idea of
man's potential to run a better mile.[4]

This rejection of the "average" as the standard of measurement,
or the use of mental illness to describe health, led Maslow to
focus on human potential and what could help healthy persons
become healthier. It also led him to examine what kept people
from achieving their potential. Goble describes many aspects of
what Maslow found characterizing persons living on the "growing
tip." The list is quite long, but it describes many of the things
that those who are "hungry" in society long for.

But, the other side of the coin, also examined by Maslow, was in what kept people from realizing their human potential. Goble listed six reasons: (1) man's instincts toward growth are weak and can be easily suppressed by other reasons; (2) the fear of playing the "hunch" or following "inner voices"—instincts—have been discouraged in the western culture; (3) many of the lower needs, safety and recognition, for example, are still greater motivators of behavior in many people; (4) the fear in adults, or doubts they have, about their own abilities and potential to be greater; (5) cultural conditioning (such as what does it mean to be male or female) repress human development; and (6) habits that are followed and make persons more brittle to new ideas and new experiences, thus causing habits to be obstacles to growth.[5]

Christian Potential

Taking the same idea of measuring Christian growth and maturity not by what the average church member can do or does, but by the "long distance runners" of the faith (something of the analogy the writer of Hebrews uses after having described the great examples of faith in the Old Testament, when he concludes, "Therefore, since we are surrounded by so great a cloud of witnesses, let us also lay aside every weight and sin which clings so closely, and let us run with perseverance the race that is set before us" Heb. 12:1), what then would Christian potential look like?

Starting with the New Testament, Jesus, the disciples, Paul, Luke, Mark, and the early church members; the early church fathers and on down to today we have those "long distance runners" who have pointed the way to Christian potential. Does this not become for us the "growing tip" of what the Christian pilgrimage can be? I could mention men and women from the past who have served as signposts along the way for me, indicating what Christian potential looks like: Augustine, Francis of Assisi, Thomas a Kempis, Martin Luther, John Calvin, Teresa of Avila, John of the Cross, Brother Lawrence, Francis de Sales, John Bunyan, Jakob Spener, William Law, John Woolman, John Wesley, John Fox, Soren Kierkegaard, Dietrich Bonhoeffer, Evelyn Underhill, Sam Shoemaker, Thomas Kelly, Thomas Merton, Walter

Rauschenbusch, Martin Luther King, and Clarence Jordan.

Some of the long distance runners continue to be with us, such as Douglas Steere, William Stringfellow, Gordon Cosby, and Mother Theresa in Calcutta, India. You make your list of those who point you towards Christian potential as I have made mine. These are the ones who speak to me of what the call to live Christian discipleship is all about. But, as you make your list, also ask yourself, "What is the Christian potential within me, and how is it called out?"

Dealing with the Wounds and Blockages

Several years ago I was introduced to the deeper dimensions of Christian maturity and growth in a devotional retreat led by Gordon Cosby; one of those conferences that preceded the establishment of The Vineyard Conference Center three years later. At that conference on the devotional life, Cosby asked the question, "Where to you want to be in your Christian life five years from now, and what plans do you have to get there?"

Dealing, as that conference did, with the devotional life of quietness, prayer, the meditative use of Scripture, and contemplation—all new experiences for me, since I had been accustomed to just reading the Bible passage suggested for the day and then jumping under the covers—that conference started me on a pilgrimage that I have since sought to keep. But, it has led me into deeper and deeper dimensions of the Christian Faith, which was like discovering both waterfalls of undescribable beauty and at the same time the deepest cliffs dropping off into sheer nothingness; all right in my backyard, which I thought was so familiar to me. Cosby called this the "cost/promise," or "pain/joy," tension. There were new and breathtaking promises and times of joy in which the temptation to "build three tabernacles and stay there" became a real temptation. But, there were also moments of pain and cost which came as Christian potential was opened and explored.

The two dimensions of the "journey inward" (growth in self-awareness and growth in a deeper relationship with God through daily conversation with him and a daily encounter of him through the Scriptures) combined with the "journey outward" (the joining

of God in mission) brought me face to face with the dimensions
a person has to encounter in dealing with his own Christian
potential.

But, the question arises about what keeps us from realizing
our Christian potential? As Maslow found according to Goble,
persons simply did not realize their human potential. We could
lump it all together and call it sin, and say that Christian potential,
like perfection, is not attainable so, therefore, I quit! Christian
potential, no more than Maslow understood human potential, is
not to be equated with perfection. His subjects were willing to
make mistakes, but they seem to also be ready to turn around
again and again and try other directions. It is the same in Christian
potential. A person must be ready to try, to be open to the new,
to know themselves and be free to fail. Goble says of Maslow:
"Self-knowledge and self-understanding, in his opinion, are the
most important roads toward self-actualization—a process which
can be aided or thwarted by parents, teachers and the cultural
environment." [6]

The movement towards the realization of Christian potential
begins with self-understanding. As Gordon Cosby has said, "We
must begin to understand the wounds and blockages that keep
us from being free." Otherwise my Christian pilgrimage becomes
nothing more than an acting out of my own ego defenses, working
from hidden compulsive behavior, or the relinquishing of my adult
decision-making powers to an authority figure over me (and many
pastors and adult Sunday school teachers fulfill this role for us)
because of my inability to deal with my dependency feelings.

The sharing group becomes that place where people can acknowledge those things that keep them from being free, and which
hold them back from reaching out for their individual Christian
potential. Briefly I want to list eight (and there are many more)
ways which describe how unknowingly we are not free, and thus
unable to achieve our Christian potential.

(1) *Categories of security* were shared by Gordon Cosby at the
first conference he led for us in 1964. He said, you are not free
as long as: (1) you do only what the group wants you to do;
(2) you do only that which will get the desired outcome; (3) you
do only that which is reasonable or logical; and (4) you do only

that which satisfies some absentee "landlord" of your spiritual values. As Cosby presented these and explained how they had worked on him in his life, I came to recognize their hold over me, especially the last one as I began to name the persons in my life, who though not physically present, continued to tell me what I "ought" to do in terms of my spiritual growth and maturity; things that did not allow me to really be free to be instructed by God through prayer and his Scriptures.

(2) *Not "OK" feelings* have been indicated by Thomas Harris in his book, *I'm OK, You're OK*. In it Harris has described how we come to feel "not OK" about ourselves and others. I have found in small groups that people often will say, when I ask them to tell the group something they like about themselves, "I wished you had asked me to tell what I don't like about myself." The prevalence of this type of feeling is much more of a blockage than we realize. Most of us simply do not like ourselves, and Harris has helped us to understand this blockage by using a process developed by Eric Berne called "transactional analysis," which is nothing more than a process to look at the transactions we have with persons and why we relate to them the way we do. In another book, *Games People Play*, from this same school of psychological studies Eric Berne talked about "games people play" with each other as a way of human interaction. Such games as "WAHM" (Why does this always happen to me?), "Kick Me," "I'm Only Trying to Help," and the marriage games of "I've Got You in a Corner Now," and "Courtroom" are ways that Berne pointed out the blockages to free, open, and honest communication between persons. Only as we come to recognize these as blockages can we come to have authentic interpersonal community.

(3) *Living behind my masks* is another way of living without being authentic and being open to Christian potential. John Powell in two little books, *Why Am I Afraid to Tell You Who I Am?*, and, *Why Am I Afraid to Love?*, examines this way of living. Speaking of "masks" as ego-defense mechanisms, which we all use to some extent or another, though the real problem comes in not recognizing our use of them, he says:

Rather than expose a self which we imagine to be inadequate or ugly, we instinctively build walls. . . . To the extent that we experience scars of anxiety, guilt, and inferiority feelings, we are tempted to wear masks, to act roles. We do not trust or accept ourselves enough to be ourselves. These walls and masks are measures of self-defense, and we will live behind our walls and wear our masks as long as they are needed. While it may seem to be a safer life behind these facades, it is also a lonely life. We cease to be authentic, and as persons we starve to death. . . . When we resort to acting out roles or wearing masks there is no possibility of human and personal growth. We are simply not being ourselves, and we cannot emerge in an atmosphere of growth. We are merely performing on a stage. When the curtain drops after our performance we will remain the same immature persons that we were when the curtain went up at the beginning of the act." [7]

(4) *We have all been wounded* to some degree and at some time in our life. This is another way of saying that there are wounds and blockages that keep us from being free to fulfill our Christian potential. Both the fact of our wounded condition and the possibility of our recognition of having been wounded and, therefore, becoming "wounded healers," is found in a book by Henri Nouwen *The Wounded Healer*. Nouwen, though he was ·writing to vocational church ministers, touches on the potential of each Christian to recognize his wounds of loneliness, isolation, separation, alienation, guilt, feelings of inferiority, dependency, having been told to "amount to something," and "grow up," "don't cry" (for men), and "don't think" (for women). He said that each of us as "the wounded healer (is) the one who must look after his own wound but at the same time be prepared to heal the wounds of others." He continues: "Making one's wounds a source of healing, therefore, does not call for a sharing of superficial personal pains, but for a constant willingness to see one's own pain and suffering as rising from the depth of the human condition which all men share." The way a person does this is not to create the illusion that "wholeness can be given by one to another. It is healing because it does not take away the loneliness and the pain of another, but invites him to recognize on a level where it can be shared." [8] This sharing, Nouwen calls hospitality, a creation of enough space in your life to share another's wounds, thus becoming the person who not only has been wounded, and recognizes his wounds, but has enough space in his life to both

recognize the wounds in another's life, and to share with them in their wounds. This gets very close to what sharing groups, and mission groups in an even greater depth, are all about.

(5) *The unblessed child* has been written about by Myron Madden in his book, *The Power to Bless.* Using the biblical study of Jacob and Esau, Madden explores the power of not being the blessed child in the household to influence our later behavior as we seek the recognition and blessings that were denied us in our childhood. He demonstrates how not being blessed during childhood has to alter our capacity for Christian growth and maturity. The way to blessing, which many of us need, is to isolate and banish "our inner demons of fear, anxiety, and guilt" for that would leave us prey to worse demons of hate, discord and division which would consume us. The way of blessing is to identify and name, the places of our lack of blessing and then to accept the affirmation and acceptance of those who can bless us today.

Whoever brings acceptance in a total way brings healing. Whoever cannot accept affirmation from another cannot be healed. Whoever shuts himself off from sharing his deeper self imposes on himself a kind of isolation or banishment from healing. In seeking to work things out "by himself" one can only revolve from self-hate to self-pity and back again. A genuine self-acceptance must be started at some point outside the self; it must come from another self who has been able to turn to accept healing from his own brokenness.[9]

(6) *Sex-role limitations* have described men as hard, nonemotional, unfeeling persons of thought and action; and women as emotional, dependent on intuition and feeling for direction, persons who cannot understand philosophical discussions, and are not decisive in decision-making (they are always making up their mind or changing it at the last minute.) These stereotypes of "maleness" and "femaleness" have also not allowed persons of both sexes to be free to be intuitive persons as well as thinking persons. It has robbed persons of Christian potential, for some of the earliest Christian leaders were women who had been freed to fulfill their Christian potential. It has kept men from showing warmth and affection, for this was supposedly not "manly."

(7) *Compulsive behavior,* which unknowingly pushes us to "have

to" do things, thus increasing the "oughts" in our lives and dimin-
ishing the capacity for us to act out our lives from a sense of
"giftness," is another one of those blockages that keeps us from
being free to fulfill our Christian potential. The man who hoards
socks as an adult because he didn't have enough as a boy; the
woman who continues to buy more and more objects for her house
in order to overcome the misery of her early home life in the
small town in which she grew up; the person who must speak
up on every issue in every group and demonstrate his intelligence
because he never got beyond the fifth grade in school; these and
other things are signs of our compulsive behavior. They are indica-
tors of a deep need to "prove" something, either to ourselves
or to others. It is another place where we become aware of the
blockages of Christian potential.

(8) *Our many selves* is the way Elizabeth O'Connor has described
a way to sum up the blockages and wounds that keep us from
being free in her book by the same name. The recognition that
there are many selves residing within us at the same time comes
through self-preservation and self-awareness. This is the reason
that this aspect of the "journey inward" becomes so important
if we are going to be free enough to realize our Christian potential;
to come to that place where we are free enough to be led by
God, and not by the pulls and tugs of our own wounds and
blockages. O'Connor gives many guides for the identification of
the many selves that make up our lives, all of which aim at the
"naming" of those selves, not their elimination. Also, getting
enough distance from these selves as they are identified, as an
observor of my own behavior, allows me to get in touch with
the plurality that is within me, and to begin that journey towards
the integration of our many selves around the "Self which is in
the Lord."

Thus, eight ways, and there are many more, in which we become
painfully aware of what keep us from being free to achieve
Christian potential. It is only by the grace of God, a gift from
him, that Christian potential is achieved in the first place. Therefore, the dealing with self-awareness in a sharing group becomes
an experience of God's grace administered to us. As many of these
have said above, it is through another that both the awareness

of the blockages occurs, and the healing takes place. And, this is the one point that I would underscore and repeat many times to those in sharing groups; don't try the opening up of self-awareness on your own! It's too full of danger, and the healing power of Christ is administered through others—this is part of the humility of Christian community that I must learn—I can't heal myself. This is the failure of motivation success schemes which promise that each of us can be a "self-made person." In the church, the community of God's new people, there are no self-made or self-healers. We are all made and healed in community. In the sharing group growth takes place through the ministry of others.

One other word about freedom. Many have cautioned, you never get free; it's a relative thing. Thomas Merton in *Contemplative Prayer* said that those obstacles may have very deep roots in our character and in fact we may eventually learn that a whole lifetime will barely be sufficient for their removal. But, one of the dimensions of growth in Christian potential is found in self-awareness in a sharing group.

Daily Depth Encounter with God

The second dimension of being free to fulfill my Christian potential is a daily depth encounter with God. There are two aspects to this daily encounter, which Brother Lawrence called simply "practicising the presence of God" so that 'he is as real to me when I am scrubbing my pots and pans as when I am in church.' [10] This dimension of the "journey inward" recognizes the immanence of God, though it takes seriously the other understanding of God as the "Holy Other." But, taking seriously a daily encounter with God in depth, through a time of quietness, meditative use of the Scripture, prayer, meditation, and contemplation, says that in order to be really free to achieve what God intends for me in terms of my Christian potential, I have to be in touch with God's plans and directions, and know how to join him in his mission of reconciliation to the brokenness of the world. For too many of us, our encounter with him is not only not *daily*, but not with any serious depth. We reserve those times of encounter with him for periods of crisis in our life, and our prayers become, then, only the prayer of petition or intercession. Thus, our encounter with God (either through prayer or his Scriptures) remains superficial like our encounter with ourselves or other persons.

Fear seems to be the greatest obstacle, not only in coming to know myself in self-awareness, but also in spending time in a daily depth encounter with God. I am afraid I will find out something about myself which I do not want to know; I am afraid that I will hear something in my encounter with God that I don't want to hear; I am afraid that I may be asked to make some changes in my life, and I am not sure that I really want that; I am afraid that if I, like Peter, ask the Lord to allow me really to launch out into an unknown area of faith and ask him to allow me to "walk on water," he will invite me to come on out! Fear really has to be dealt with as one becomes aware of what Christian potential can open up in our lives. But, the recognition of this fear that keeps us back from a deeper journey inward in a daily encounter with God demonstrates the relationship between self-awareness and a deeper daily encounter with God.

Many of the blockages and wounds that we have described above are those things that keep me from being open to a deeper walk with the Lord, which is what we say we all want. So both of these dimensions of the journey inward have to be dealt with simultaneously if we are really to be free enough to be able to hear the still small voice; to play the hunches of where God would have us be ministering today; to be able to have eyes that really see and ears that really hear the points of brokenness and infidelity. This is what makes the journey inward very costly.

Most of us have grown up on "inspirational books," which we have equated with "devotional books." But, the difference is very large. For the most part, inspirational books are books that have told us how to be better Christians and urged us on to more successful behavior. In a sense, they have been, by and large, the success motivation books of the Protestant Christian tradition. They have told us what should be done and have compounded our guilt because we were not quite up to it. In contrast, the devotional classics have been written by persons who were writing of their struggles with living the life of discipleship in depth so that devotional classics have become for many guideposts for those who were seeking to be free enough to be led in their search into the unknown of faith, and not urged on by another's formula for instant Christian success.

The daily depth encounter with God is of that quality. It is a daily encounter with God into deeper and deeper levels of our being as we encounter his presence and listen to his words as it ministers to us in both pointing out our infidelities, and affirming our victories. This daily depth encounter, for many, has some definite parts to it, though each person should be free enough to find the combination of these parts that best communicate this daily encounter with God to him. And, the amount of time spent in his daily depth encounter with God must be determined according to the "critical minimum," as Cosby calls it, which will allow that person to function as an inward person, one who can see, hear, and discern both God's will to wholeness and freedom, and then live at that point where we encounter daily the will of the world to death. For many this daily depth encounter is thirty minutes a day, for others at least an hour or more, but each one must find that point below which he is no longer able to function as a discerning child of God. The time and place of this daily depth encounter is left up to the person to decide, the only guideline being that it should be done each day at the same time and with a predetermined amount of time, which can be increased if necessary.

The daily depth encounter with God begins with a "centering down," or an awareness of the quiet center out of which life must be lived if the "pollution of things and opportunities" does not overcome us in their diversified demands on us. It is in the "quiet center" that priorities are determined and a preparedness is made for a devotional encounter with the living God. But, because we are so busy, listening to so many demands made on us from within us, and by duties and oughts outside of us, we fail to stop the "wheels" long enough to spend time in the quiet center where we can listen and be heard by One who had concern for the sparrows and the lillies of the field.

And we are unhappy, uneasy, strained, oppressed and fearful we shall be shallow. For over the margins of life comes a whisper, a faint call, a premonition of richer living which we know we are passing by. Strained by the very mad pace of our daily outer burdens, we are further strained by an inward uneasiness, because we have hints that there is a way of life vastly richer and deeper than all this hurried existence, a life of unhurried serenity and peace and power. If only we could slip over into that Center! If only we could find the Silence which is the ource of sound! [11]

That a quiet center does exist at some level has to become a deep conviction for us before we are willing to spend time in it. There are hints and clues of its existence and we know people who seem to constantly live out of this quiet center, for "they are busy carrying their full load as well as we, but without any chafing of the shoulders with the burden, with quiet joy and springing step. Surrounding the trifles of their daily life is an aura of infinite peace and power and joy. We are so strained and tense, with our burdened lives; they so poised and at peace." [12] What's the difference? Kelly and others are convinced that it is the living of life out of this "quiet center" amid the swirlings of all of life around; and this means taking time to live life out of this center rather than the demands that come tugging at each of us with their oughts. But time to do this has to become a life-style changing priority. Michel Quoist has expressed it in a prayer this way:

> I'd like to pray, but I haven't time.
> You understand, Lord, they simply haven't the time.

But, then Quoist goes on to say:

> You give each one time to do what you want him to do.
> But you must not lose time
>   waste time,
>   kill time,
> For this is a gift that you give us,
> But a perishable gift,
> A gift that does not keep.
> Lord, I have time
> I have plenty of time. [13]

A willingness to step out into life from the "quiet center" and then to live at the juncture of brokenness in a wounded society with eyes that can see, and ears that can hear, and a willingness to be led calls forth in each of us Christian potential. Roman Guardini said: "Prayer must begin with this collectedness." [14] So the journey into daily encounter with God begins with a time of quietness, collectedness, a centering down, where we push back all thoughts, plans and interruptions that would distract us, and prepare for an encounter with the living God.

Prepared for this deeper encounter with God, we now turn to the Scriptures to let them speak to us meditatively. There are important places for intellectual study of the Bible content taught at the foot of a good Bible teacher so that we may understand the correct interpretation of its message. There are also places where we use the Bible in a relational Bible study fashion in order to recreate the Bible story so that it becomes not only the story of persons who lived two thousand years ago, but my story; a picture of my Christian pilgrimage now. But, there is a place for the Bible to be used in a meditative fashion, and that is what should follow a time of quietness and being centered down. For many this will be a new experience, for we've tended to think of the Bible as a set of rules (going back to the "do's and don't's" measurement of Christian maturity and growth) or a book of magic wisdom that could be opened randomly and with a pointed finger solve problems of direction for the day.

When we encounter the Bible as a record of God's people who have been seeking, sometimes rightly and sometimes falsely, an understanding of what it means to be the people of God, then it becomes open to us at a deeper dimension. At that level it can speak to us about the same problems others have encountered as they sought to understand what it means to be free to fulfill Christian potential.

Cosby, employing Lynn Radcliffe's guide in using the Scripture meditatively,[15] has helped me to find a way to do this. I am sure there are others, but I share this one for it has been meaningful to me and others with whom I have shared it since discovering it several years ago. There are four "P's" which guide us after being centered down: preparing, picturing, pondering, and praying. The first step is to *prepare* a passage of Scripture, preferably the day before so as not to interrupt the time of devotions with searching for a suitable Scripture selection. It should be a brief passage that will be studied (a word, a phrase, or a short selection). Also, in preparation you pray consciously that the Holy Spirit will come and open up that passage for you and allow it to live for you. You also pray that you will be able to enter into a real dialogue with Christ concerning the passage you have meditated over.

Secondly, you use all your past study of the passage to to *picture* in your mind just exactly what is found in that which you are studying. If it is the story of the disciples who had caught no fish and Jesus asked them to cast their nets on the other side one more time, you try to smell the sea air, hear the nets being drawn up and cast out, and the splashing of the fish as they are brought up out of the water. You "picture" all that you ever thought or remembered about the passage and reconstruct the feelings and the scene itself.

Thirdly, you move from the use of imagination to actually place yourself in the presence of Jesus himself through that word, phrase or passage, and you say to him, "Jesus, what do you have to say to me through this passage?" This is the hardest part of the meditative use of Scripture because this is the point where you ask God to speak to you through this passage, come what may, change what ever may have to change. This is threatening for it is Christ confronting me through his word, and it may be that what God tells me through his word may change my life! At this point I am no longer just using the passage I mentioned above. To illustrate this, the command to the fisherman to cast their nets on the other side may lead me to hear him say to me that I need to do again a task that I have done several times and that the next time the catch will be abundant. Or, it may be that I hear him say to me that I have been unwilling to go back into deep water (a place of particular difficulty for me) for I am still "wounded" from the bitter experience of my past failure, or the insensitive ridicule of those who laughed at me; and I refuse each time he asks me to launch out into the deep. At this point Christ is in our presence and speaking to us about what it is he would have us do. This is the work of *pondering* on the passage.

Lastly, we slip over into the time of *prayer*, for already we've been conversing with God and he with us, and this is what prayer is all about, a conversation between two friends. And, as we continue to pray we wait sometimes to hear what he will say to us, and we speak to him about our feelings whatever they are, even the hostile ones, for we must be honest in our conversation with God. Unless we are honest in our conversation with God we are not going to have any reality in our prayer life, and we are not going to talk with him about our lives as they really are with an all-seeing Father. During this time we lift up to him those persons for whom we are called on to remember in intercessory prayer.

For some, this last area of meditation (prayer) as they have practiced it over the years, has led them to come to that point where prayer language becomes very limited in a time of adoration. Many of the saints simply prayed with the few words, "Jesus Christ, Son of God, have mercy on me a sinner," or simply repeated the name of "Jesus" over and over, for words have failed to express all that they felt in their time of prayer. Beyond meditation there are times of contemplation in which a person seeks to put everything out of his mind and to concentrate entirely on God and him alone. Merton calls it a "deeper and simpler intuitive form of receptivity."

Prayer, in the terms described above means that we have redefined the life of prayer, which for many is only reserved for crisis. Then the only prayer that is prayed is the prayer of petition—Lord help me out of this spot, or heal this person, or rescue me from this trouble. That type of praying sees prayer as a way to "get something done" rather than a resting in the presence of God. Merton said, "It is a distortion of the contemplative life to treat it as if the contemplative concentrated all his efforts on getting graces and favors from God for others and for himself."

If we are involved only in our surface existence, in externals and in the trivial concerns of our ego, we are untrue to Him and to ourselves. To reach a true awareness of Him as well as ourselves, we have to renounce our selfish and limited self and enter into a whole new kind of existence, discovering an inner center of motivation and love which makes us see ourselves and everything else in an entirely new light. Call it faith, call it (at a more advanced stage) contemplative illumination, call it the sense of God or even mystical union: all these are different aspects and levels of the same kind of realization: the awakening to a new awareness of ourselves in Christ, created in Him, redeemed by Him, to be transformed and glorified in and with Him. In Blake's words, the "doors of perception" are opened and all life takes on a completely new meaning: the real sense of our own existence, which is normally veiled and distorted by the routine distractions of an alienated life, is now revealed in a central intuition. . . . This peculiar, brilliant focus is, . . . a contemplative knowledge, a fruit of living and realizing faith, a gift of the spirit.[16]

What then is the purpose of prayer, meditative use of the Scriptures, and contemplation—a daily depth encounter with God—in achieving the fulfillment of our Christian potential? Again, Merton has summed it up for me as he talks about the purpose of prayer: "*Prayer* then means yearning for the simple presence of God. for a personal understanding of his word, for knowledge of his will and for capacity to hear and obey him. It is thus something much more than uttering petitions for good things external to our own deepest concerns." [17]

How much time each day, again, depends on what it takes for you to achieve those goals that Merton mentions. For many it has to be a minimum of thirty minutes a day, for others an hour or more. What is important is that as we encounter God on a daily basis through prayer and the Scriptures we come to have a sense of his continuing presence throughout the day; and we may find times when the passage we meditated on that day continues to have new and richer meanings as the day progresses. It also makes us sensitive to the unplanned occasions of ministry and witness which the Holy Spirit gives us as he has prepared persons for our ministry. This time makes us more in tune with the nudgings of the Holy Spirit to move with God in certain directions as he did with Philip in attaching him to the Ethiopian eunuch to interpret the Isaiah passage; or the ministry of availability that Ananias performed on Paul's eyes so that he could see again; or the ministry of Peter being available to Gentile Cornelius in order that the good news might be opened to them also.

Lastly, this journey inward should make me more and more

aware of my gifts for ministry. Elizabeth O'Connor has done a good job in writing about the discovery of personal gifts for mission in *The Eighth Day of Creation*. In it she has indicated a process for the discovery of gifts for ministry, which will be essential as persons move from sharing groups into mission groups. But the calling forth of gifts should be explored as persons enter into these two dimensions of the journey inward.

Conclusion

Sharing groups are places where "hungry people" gather to share at deeper levels of their being, in an atmosphere of openness and honesty, caring and sharing, where deeper dimensions of the Christian pilgrimage can be explored, and new understandings tried on as a new depth of the Christian discipleship is incorporated into our lives.

Sharing groups are first steps for hungry people looking for growth in Christian potential. Bruce Larson calls it in his book by the same name, "living on the growing edge": "When we are open to God's leading, we find that He pushes us into those relationships that threaten us most and in which we feel least comfortable. . . . Those who are living on the growing edge with God are open to hearing and experiencing things that may seem strange and 'unorthodox.' " [18] Others have said that Christian potential is being open to the ministry of God's "holy discomfort," in which he nudges us into new and exciting dimensions. But, sharing groups do not push people into growth, they simply allow, in the sharing process, the ministry of God's Holy Spirit to call forth hunger, and for wholeness to be administered.

Thus, sharing groups in the church are preparatory structures for opening up new dimensions of Christian discipleship which can be more fully explored in in-depth study structures and later in mission groups. As a preparatory structure, they serve the purpose of focusing around one particular area of interest or concern of the participants, but they move on to introduce other dimensions of Christian growth as the group is willing to commit themselves to them. Two of these dimensions of the journey inward have been mentioned above: dealing with the wounds and blockages; and a daily depth encounter with God.

Sharing groups become effective for persons who have come to the conclusion that the problems with themselves and the congregations of which they are part are not found in "externals" but within. As long as we assign the problems we face to the need to have a better program for the youth, or a better place to worship, or I need a more "meaningful" job, or I need a better house, or more furniture, or my children need to be better behaved—to externals—then we will not search for the answers to the real problems within ourselves. Changed circumstances will not improve the real source of the problems which lie within us. The reason the Bible is so difficult to understand for most of us is that it was written by persons who were inward persons; they had grappled with themselves as they faced the call of God to pilgrimage.

The call of God that soon becomes apparent in sharing groups is that God is asking us to take our hands off our lives and the very life of the church itself in order for him to do something quite unusual and unexpected with it. John Haughey has said: "The joy of the kingdom belongs to those to whom it has been given to inhale the truth about themselves. . . . The limitations that are imposed . . . come not as much from our sinfulness, I suspect, as from our unwillingness to entertain the view of ourselves that God has of us." [19] The call to Christian potential is to be free enough, both in self-awareness of the blockages and wounds that keep me from being free, as well as in living at a daily deep encounter with him, to be led of His Holy Spirit into those new and deeper dimensions of the faith that are uniquely mine. Sharing groups provide the preparatory structures for the beginning of that pilgrimage.

1. Thomas A. Harris, *I'm OK, You're OK* (New York: Harper & Row, 1969) p. 60.
2. Leslie, *op. cit.*, pp. 158-59.
3. Frank Goble, *The Third Force* (New York: Pocket Books, 1970), pp. 15-16.
4. *Ibid.*, p. 24.
5. *Ibid.*, pp. 60-61.
6. *Ibid.*, p. 62.
7. John Powell, *Why Am I Afraid to Love?* (Chicago: Argus Communications, 1972), pp. 52-53.

8. Nouwen, *op. cit.*, pp. 84-94, passim.

9. Myron C. Madden, *The Power to Bless* (Nashville: Abingdon Press, 1970), p. 141.

10. Brother Lawrence, *The Practice of the Presence of God* (Westwood, N.J.: Fleming H. Revell Co., 1958).

11. Thomas R. Kelly, *A Testament of Devotion* (New York: Harper & Row, 1941), p. 115.

12. *Ibid.*, p. 116.

13. Michel Quoist, *Prayers* (New York: Sheed & Ward, 1963), p. 76.

14. Quoted in O'Connor, *Search for Silence*, p. 129.

15. Lynn J. Radcliffe, *Making Prayer Real* (Nashville: Abingdon Press, 1952).

16. Thomas Merton, *Contemplation in a World of Action* (New York: Image Books, 1971), p. 176.

17. Merton, *Comtemplative Prayer*, p. 67.

18. Larson, *Living on the Growing Edge*, pp. 19-20.

19. John C. Haughey, *The Conspiracy of God: The Holy Spirit in Men* (New York: Doubleday, 1973), p. 93.

6 How to Get Started

"Hey, this has been great! How can I get this going in my church?" These words are often heard at the end of a retreat, a renewal conference, or a lay weekend. Those who say this have just encountered a group experience in which certain of their needs have been met, and they wish to continue what has been started.

Care needs to be exercised at this point in order to insure that inspiration doesn't exceed preparation. The gap that exists between the desire to start a sharing group and the practical knowledge of how to get started and follow through is sometimes a big one. How do you locate others who share your hunger or enthusiasm? How many should there be in the group? Who will lead it once it is started? Where will you meet? These are just a few of the questions that have to be answered as you begin a sharing group.

Inviting Persons to Sharing Groups

There may not be *one* best way to begin a sharing group, but basic understandings about sharing groups indicate that some ways work better than others. Let's say that you have been to a retreat, a renewal conference, or a lay weekend and have experienced the value of a small sharing group. You feel that you could benefit from a continuing group experience. Where do you go from there? What are some of the ways you could gather people about you? You could share your experience with your pastor, enlisting his help in enlisting group members. He could do this with an announcement from the pulpit. Or, you could use the church bulletin, or church newsletter, to reach those who might be interested. A third method might be to make an announcement in all of the adult departments at the church.

However, I have personally found the above suggestions to be the least effective in enlisting small group members. Therefore, let me offer some other suggestions, which seem to be more effective. One, have a "Serendipity Party" in which you invite friends to your home, share with them your own experience, lead them in some group experiences, and find out who is interested in starting a group. Another way is personally to invite friends who seem to share common interests in personal growth, involvement in missions, and a need for fellowship to be a part of the group. This is done on a one-to-one invitation basis. The third suggestion is also grounded in the personal approach. Look about you. Be open and sensitive to all of those around you. Who are those who are sharing their joys, their hurts, their frustrations, their desire to have real fellowship? These are prime candidates. I have found that there are many people like this around who would love to be part of a small group of people who are looking for new and deeper dimensions of personal experience with God and others.

The difference between the first and the second set of suggestions rests in the personal invitation and the starting with persons who are invited because of some personal need. General announcements rarely, if ever, get the job done. You will find out that you will have better results in enlisting if you take someone by the elbow and say, "Hey, let me share a dream with you."

The First Few Meetings of a Sharing Group

Lyman Coleman has done a real service for all who want to be involved in small sharing groups with his personal involvement and knowledge of small groups.[1] He has recognized that a group of people become a community only through sharing with one another. He has stated the purpose of small sharing groups to be the development of love, trust, and acceptance for one another. This love, trust, and acceptance isn't achieved in a few minutes. You can't really love me until you know me; and you can't know me until I tell you something about myself. This telling you of myself is done a little at a time, in a manner that is safe and acceptable.

Therefore, it is necessary, as Coleman points out, for a sharing group to spend its first several sessions simply building group relationships. The number of weekly meetings it takes to build community vary, but it usually takes four to five sessions of one and a half hours each. This may mean four or five weeks of meeting with nothing on the agenda but the building of relationships between the group members. Or, this may be done in a weekend retreat set aside only for building relationships.

For many, it is hard to imagine that it would take that much time to build relationships among eight or ten persons. But, if you multiply that number of persons times the thirty to sixty minutes per person it takes for me to tell you who I am, then you see the time needed to build relationships which have any depth to them. Taking time to build relationships is the first step towards building a sharing group.

Coleman points out that the first error of many small groups is to assume that a group can go immediately (or even sometimes too quickly) to the study of a book, or the accomplishment of a task, without doing the necessary work of building group relationships. His view, which he calls a dynamic view, says that a sharing group needs to spend its first sessions primarily in building group relationships, then the study of content, or the performance of a task, take on new meaning. But, study and task performance should not be rushed into too soon, before some depth of relationships have been established.

The four steps Coleman outlines in building relationships in a sharing group are: history giving; affirmation; goal setting; and *koinonia*.[2] These steps must be taken in sequence, and, if properly and seriously worked with, will encourage the emergence of love, trust, and acceptance which is the essential climate in which a sharing group will do the rest of its work.

Step One

Coleman calls this "history giving." Here the members tell about themselves in terms of their past, where they were born, something about family relationships, childhood dreams, school experiences, and significant people. They also share something about themselves in terms of the present; what exciting things are happening in their lives today. Finally, they share something about the future. Where they would like to be five years from now.

To allow each member to share this kind of information takes time, but it is time well spent. In fact, this is probably the most important time in the life of the group. This is setting the stage for all that is to follow. You not only give information about yourself, you also receive information about the other members of the group. The more you know, the better equipped you are to understand the other person.

Step Two

The second step is called "affirmation." Here you focus on your strengths and the strengths of other members of the group. What do you like about the other group members? What is it that you like about yourself? You need to take time and tell each member what it is that you like about him/her. You also need to hear what the others like about you. This is healing in itself. One of the greatest problems that we have today is the inability to like ourselves; to receive affirmation from others; or to tell others, "Hey, I like this about you." For some reason, we find it much easier to be critical, to turn aside positive feelings. The second step allows a person to grow in another dimension of himself. At this stage the information flow is two-way; both to the group and from the group to me.

Step Three

"Goal setting" is the next step. Once mutual acceptance and trust have taken place, and the group members feel good about each other and themselves, it is time to move on to goal setting. Goal setting is very similar to history giving in that personal information is offered by each member of the group. The difference between steps one and three is that goal setting goes much deeper. The focus now is on deep hurts and areas where you feel you need to grow and develop. Relationships with peers, family, and friends dominate the conversation. This is a difficult, but fruitful, time in the life of a group. Nevertheless, it has been made easier because of the care and concern that has developed through the two previous steps.

Step Four

Koinonia! Fellowship! Community! Support! That is what the

final step is all about. Through the presence of the Holy Spirit
and the caring, healing love of the group members, unity takes
place. The journey has been worth it. Now is the time for celebration. Wow! A new level of group relationship has been reached;
and, as Coleman says, "the facilitation of the group has shifted
from an outside control, to a mysterious new control system where
the Spirit is free to move in and through the members of the
group." When a group does achieve this level of community,
no one has to point it out; all know it. It is a time when you
care, I mean really care, and you love and are loved through
Christ.

I want to recommend the use of the "Serendipity Series" of
group workbooks by Lyman Coleman for guidance in building
group relationships through these four steps. I believe they are
the best materials available for assisting a sharing group in the
first four or five sessions. When I was responsible for convening
a sharing group in the past, I tried to structure the first four
or five weekly sessions around these four steps in group building,
after which the sharing group was on its own to find its particular
direction for the remaining weeks of the term (eight to twelve
weeks). This means that the first four or five weeks are predetermined towards the goal of group building, and after that (four
to eight weeks) the group decides on its continuing purpose and
direction.

During the first week (or the first four or five weeks), I used
one, or several, of Coleman's workbooks to find games, relational
Bible studies, or inductive Bible studies, which would help the
group move through a time of history-giving; telling who they
are. That's all I would do at that first meeting. But, it takes time
for each person to share who they are, either through a game
approach, or a relational Bible study, or an inductive study.
Someone may begin to get nervous and say, "When are we going
to get on with the real study, or get down to business?" But,
remember, that is the business of the first four or five sessions,
building relationships. It's very costly in time and personal involvement, but there are no shortcuts here.

The second week, if you have had time for each person to
share personally his history the previous week, then I would move

on to "affirmation activities;" then each week thereafter to "goal-setting" activities; and finally to "celebration or *koinonia* activities." I would plan activities for each week based on what I had been able to get accomplished the preceding week, thus slowly allowing enough time for each step to be completely finished, before moving on to the next. However, don't bog down in one step just because you are getting such a great enjoyment out of it. Move on, for the next step is equally full of rewarding experiences.

After Building Relationships, What?

When a sharing group has reached step four in group building relationships, it has some basis on which to make a decision concerning its continuing purpose for the remaining weeks of its existence. Sharing groups at this point have formed around various purposes: prayer groups, Bible study groups, dialogue groups, spiritual growth groups, interest groups, fellowship groups, renewal groups, searching groups, marriage groups, singles groups, home groups, growth cells, family groups, student groups, and vocational groups.

The list could go on and on for there are many names for sharing groups which churches have used. The most important thing is not the name, however, but the focus of the group. Group names can be, and at times often are, misleading. For this reason, what the group members are looking for in a sharing group in the church needs to be clear at this point in the life of the group. In other words, the sharing group needs to decide on what will meet individual personal needs at that particular point of their own Christian growth.

But, now let's examine briefly a few of the types of sharing groups.

Searching group.—Early in my seminary training I began searching for answers, some personal, some theological, but all practical. I had intense feelings about the church and about my role as a minister. I was not questioning my commitment to the church but rather how I could best fulfill this commitment. So, I began a search with others who were also hurting; persons who had the same questions and needs. I found support during this time with that group which helped me discover the answers I needed then.

Interest group.—The interest group of which I was a member at another time focused on the devotional classics. John Bunyan, Thomas Merton, St. Augustine, and Ignatius Loyola were but a few of the men that we studied together. At that time, I had just discovered the classics and desired to talk with someone else about their meaning and help for today. To pursue this interest was most meaningful to me. The interest group formed around one particular subject; the devotional classics. Once this area had been explored to our satisfaction, the group disbanded.

Interest groups can form around any topic, or book, or project, Once a particular area has been studied, the same group may contract to go directly to another area of interest, or disband, as we did.

Renewal group.—This group tends to be a combination of several types of groups. It can be an interest group, in that the focus is on personal ministry, commitment to God in Christ. Or, it can be a struggling group where members encounter one another through personal sharing. It can also be a group where healing happens as real caring is demonstrated to persons who hurt.

The importance in identifying these types of sharing groups is for the group to clarify its purpose for the remaining time together. There are no answers at this point, except to indicate the types of sharing groups which others have found helpful in the past. At this point the group direction must come from within the group, and because of having taken time to build relationships, it will emerge.

Who Is the Leader?

Most church groups do not need a formal leader for each session. Leadership can, and in most cases should, emerge from the group and be shared by the group members. Sure, there needs to be someone to convene the meeting for the first few times in order to get started; but, after the preliminaries are over, leadership should be rotated. Expert leadership is not necessary for most church groups. Shared leadership, with all of the members taking part, is the best approach.

Somebody has said, that in every group there is generally someone who has responsibility for: (1) input (verbal or nonverbal), (2) facilitating the meeting, and (3) receiving. As the group process takes place, every member will eventually fulfill all three functions. Thus, leadership will shift from one to the other.

From time to time certain members of the group may well be designated as the leader for particular functions, but even then the overall purpose is to create an atmosphere where all will feel free to take part, sometimes as leader/teacher and sometimes as follower/learner.

When and Where to Meet?

Anywhere the group wants to meet is just about the best answer. There was a time when some thought that any place was okay except the church itself. Thus, many living rooms became meeting places for small groups. But, that time has passed and even church facilities are being used for the meeting of small groups. The group will determine the best place to meet after looking at all of the factors involved.

The church facilities sometimes offer some things which a home cannot, such as nursery services for small children and ample parking. Also, persons are away from many of the things that can distract them from the group meeting, such as the telephone, children, and visitors who happen to stop by. On the other hand, meetings in homes provide a warm, informal atmosphere in familiar surroundings, and snacks can be prepared and served easily. The group needs to meet in that place which best serves the needs of all the members.

When to meet also poses another question that groups need to decide. Most of us are hearing a great deal about leisure time in America today, but so far this leisure time hasn't found me. Finding time for another meeting is sometimes very difficult and requires a discipline on our part. The biggest problem most of us have is in setting priorities. I generally find time to do those things I really want to do. To be a member of a small group that meets on a continuing basis demands that persons set priorities. Otherwise, it is easy to find yourself too involved in other things to be a meaningful member.

My wife and I have found that the best time for us to meet in a small group is on a week night, after the evening meal is over and the children taken care of for the evening. This frees us to concentrate on the group. It also frees us to be really present to our children while they are awake during week and on the weekends.

Deciding on when to meet can very well consume the greater part of the first meeting. There will always be one or two persons who will, because of schedules, have to withdraw. One of the interesting factors which emerges during this time of deciding on a time to meet concerns television. Before long you know who watches what and who won't miss what on the tube.

How Long Should a Group Meet?

This question needs to be looked at in two parts. One concerns the time in terms of minutes, the other concerns time in terms of weeks or months.

First, how long should each session of the group meet? My personal preference is one and one-half to two hours—and not a minute more. It is better to go home wishing you could stay a little longer than dreading the meeting that one never knows when it will end. This entire time should be given over to group process. In other words, no lengthy breaks should break the session up, such as the serving of refreshments that could well wait until after the session. Otherwise, by the time the group really gets to rolling, the time is up. Also, unnecessary activities make it difficult for the group to return to the level of sharing that they had previously reached. While it may be absolutely necessary for a member to occasionally have to be moving in and out, the majority should stay with the group until the time is over.

One of the most dissatisfying group experiences I ever had came when the designated leader interrupted a member who was sharing deeply to announce a coffee and doughnut break. The group never reached the intense level it had before. Not only that, the person who was sharing never felt free again to share at that level. How would you like to be interrupted in the middle of sharing your experience about an impending divorce for coffee? Think about it and plan your time accordingly.

The second part of the time question concerns the life of the group. How long should a group continue before it breaks up? This question must be answered before the group really goes very far. My personal preference for new groups is to meet once a week for eight to twelve weeks. After this time, the group can break up, at which time they can: (1) decide to continue for another eight to twelve weeks; (2) join another sharing group; (3) move to the in-depth study structure; or (4) drop out. There are several reasons for this time limitation. It may be that one or more members of the group are not really sure they want to be a part of such sharing groups. And, it is easier to commit themselves for a short period of time so they feel that they are not signing up for the rest of their lives. In other words, they need to see an end in sight. Second, some groups never "jell"; that is, they never work out even in twelve weeks. To continue them is sheer torture. Finally, the terminal date gives the members an honorable out; they don't have to "quit" the group.

How Many Should Be in a Group?

The size of a group is very important. Given the time and the number in the group everyone should have an opportunity to share. A group that is too large to allow for this means that some people remain only observers, which destroys the group process. I have found that eight to twelve is a good number for most church groups. There should be enough members in the group to keep anyone from feeling too obvious, or feeling that if he doesn't say something, nothing will be said. On the other hand the group should not be so large that members can hide and not be a participating member of the group. One factor which may limit the group size is the meeting place. Some living rooms are very small and, if you crowd fifteen people in them, you can have real fellowship!

An Open or Closed Group?

The question that every group has to deal with at some point is: Will new members be allowed to join after the group has begun? This is not an easy question to answer. For several years now I have held closely to the idea of the closed group. By this

I mean that no new members are allowed to enter the group once the group has formed. This is especially true with regard to sharing groups since the level of sharing always shifts towards the superficial every time a new individual enters, and the questions of the risk of honesty and trust have to be renegotiated. A mission group, however, can allow new persons to join at fixed times during the year; but special procedures have to be devised for this which will be examined later.

Conclusion

Now you've found out some things about how to enlist persons, what to do at the first meeting, the types of sharing groups, along with some of the basics of small groups. Now let's look at the "dynamics," or what happens to people in a group setting. This next chapter will help you have "eyes and ears" to hear and see all that is going on in a small group, not just what "appears" to be going on on the surface, as we examine a case study of a sharing group in action. Then, the following chapter will examine groups in terms of group dynamics, thereby giving you some handles for seeing and hearing all that goes on in groups.

Notes

1. See the "Serendipity Series" of workbooks authored by Lyman Coleman (Waco: Creative Resources, Word Publishing, Inc.).

2. Lyman Coleman, *Workbook for National Serendipity Workshops,* n.d., pp. 26-27.

7 This Is the Way We Grow—Struggle

It was 9:45 A.M. and the idea of starting a group was still running through Barbara's mind. She could remember being encouraged to start one by Ed Martin, the minister of education, who had been recently facilitating the growth of small sharing groups in the church. So Barbara had done it. She had gotten together a small group of ten women in her home two weeks earlier.

For some time Barbara had been wanting to get to know the women who were members of her church, who also lived in her same subdivision. These were also the same women with whom she and her husband found themselves occasionally together, not only in church social events, but also in civic and community affairs.

Barbara had been part of a small sharing group experience for a short time in the church led by the minister of education. Ed Martin had encouraged all those who had participated in the small group experience to find other people who would seem to be at that point in their lives where they would benefit from being part of a sharing group experience. He promised that he would continue to help them as they worked with their small groups.

So Barbara and the other group members had, under Ed's guidance, begun to invite persons whom they began to pick out to their homes to share in a small group. So, she was now getting the house ready and the coffee fixed this particular morning, for the group would be there in fifteen minutes.

The group had already met four times at Barbara's home, and this would be their fifth meeting. But, the apprehension that she was feeling was more than just starting the small group, it was over the feeling that the group didn't seem to be getting anywhere. The last time they had met the questions that they were asking were: Where are we going? What are we going to do? And, I don't know whether I'm committed to this group thing or not.

Sharon: Last time you asked me to take notes about the things we need to deal with at this meeting, and I guess the best place to begin is with this list so we can decide what we want to do from now on. We asked some questions like: Where are we going? What is going to be our focus? How long are we going to meet? Are we going to meet every week, and for how long each time? And, what about what we say here at these meetings, is it going to be held in confidence? Well, that's the list I got.

Sally: I think we need to decide first what our purpose is. You know, why are we meeting? Is this to be like a weekly social, which is all right with me. But, the last time we met I heard a lot of you down on the church and what it wasn't doing, and I'm not sure I feel that way. Are we here to talk about what is wrong, or to do something about it?

Louise: You said we were going to meet each week, Barbara, but how long? I mean how many hours each time, and how long is this group going to last?

Nancy: I want to add to the list something I felt last week, but didn't say. Are we going to study a book, meet for prayer, or what? It looks to me that about all we are doing now is being another morning coffee club, with just a new element of doing these things to get to know each other better. And, that may be all right.

Jane: Why not let's study the book of Revelation in the Bible? I heard a sermon the other night on the radio that was real interesting, and it spoke about how the Bible has predictions about the world problems that are going on around us right now. I'd like to know what the Bible says about where we are headed in our nation now.

Ann: If there is one thing, Jane, that I don't need right now it's another Bible study. I'm sorry to be that blunt, but I'm up to here with more than I can handle now. I'll tell you what I need. I need to get out of the house for a few minutes and be able to talk with someone other than my children.

Lynn: Ann, I hear you, but I am needing to be fed, also. I mean really fed spiritually. And, I think that part of what we should do here—maybe not all of it—should be some kind of devotional experience. I feel like my own devotional life is so shallow, and I simply don't know what to do.

Sharon: Now, I'm adding all this to the list, but I think we are talking more about what we are going to do, and still we haven't decided on some of these other things I have here on the list from last time, such as how long are we going to meet each time, and for how many weeks.

Barbara: Well, I thought we had decided at the first meeting that we would meet here at my home from 10:00 to 11:30 each Thursday morning and only for ten weeks, but if the group wants to meet elsewhere and open up these other questions, that's okay too. Let me tell you about the group I was in with Ed Martin down at the church . . .

Helen: I heard about that group. You studied the Bible for awhile, and then I heard that it ended up as just a group of people who sat around each week and gripped about the church.

Phyllis: I was in that group too, Helen, and I would like to know where you heard that, because the group really helped me. It was the first time I felt I could be really honest with another group of people in the church. But, I'm not going to be that honest again if everything we say here is going to be known all over the church. The reason I feel I need the support of a group like this is that I found in that other group some areas in my life in which I needed to grow. So I need a group like this to help me. But, I'm not going to do it in this group if there is no responsibility on each of our part to hold in confidence what we've said.

Barbara: You know, I think it was good the Bible study part of that group at the church ended after four weeks. And, it is true we did end up primarily sharing honestly our feelings about the church and our own Christian growth. That was what helped me the most because they were my feelings, and I felt that the persons in the group were listening to me.

A long uneasy pause fell over the group. Two critical issues of any group's development had been raised as the group searched and struggled for an on-going direction: (1) Can the members of the group really be honest about those things that really concern each member in their own Christian experience? (This is the risk of being honest.) (2) Can the members of the group really be trusted with those feelings and have confidence that what is shared honestly in the group be kept within the group? (This is the risk of trust.)

Nancy: I wasn't in the group that met with Ed Martin; and, unlike Helen, I haven't heard anything about the group, except what has been said this morning. But, Barbara, I have seen some changes in your life; though, Phyllis, I haven't known you that well to say whether you have changed or not, but I'm sure you have. But, Barbara, I felt you were getting help from somewhere. I've seen the times when you were tense and abrupt with persons at church, and it almost seemed you just wanted people to stay out of your way.

I don't know how to go about sharing very deeply; I think that's what I need the most . . . (Crying softly. There was another long period of silence in the group. Barbara reached out her hand and just placed it on Nancy's in a reassuring manner.)

But, I don't know what a Christian home should be like. I don't think I've ever known one. I didn't grow up in one, and I'm trying to make ours one, but it seems I fail, the harder I try. We can't get devotions done. My husband goes to church only occasionally, and this is beginning to affect the children. When I am in Bible study on Sunday morning, I get lost. I don't know the Bible like most of you know it, and yet I don't feel that just memorizing the Bible will do it. I tried to be a part of it, but what I need to know is how to live the Christian life.
   Silence

Louise: The other night, I was with a group of Harry's at the office, and we were having dinner together, and a few of the wives were talking about their husbands' being away from home so much traveling on their jobs. And, we are generally by ourselves most of the time while they are away, and it's lonely! I am so fed up with this kind of life, eating by myself, that I'm at the point where if Harry doesn't change jobs, I'm afraid that something is going to happen.

Phyllis: You know, I'm not a group leader, but I do know from that other group experience with Ed Martin, it is going to take a lot longer to handle what we've just heard from these two than we've got now. I remember Ed used to talk to us about the danger of someone's sharing something deeply, and then not have enough time to deal with it in the group. I would like to suggest something that we can do. Though, this will not answer the questions we've heard here just now, it is about all that I know to do right now. Let's hold hands around the circle, and I'd like to pray for all of us in support of these two who have shared very openly their struggles.

As is often the case, the sharing of one person makes it easier for another to "risk" it. It was good that one person was sensitive enough to "bind up" the wounds at that point, but the awareness of time helped to keep it from going to the point that the group could not be able to minister adequately to the two persons.

Sharon: I've got a question. We haven't got much time left; but, while Barbara gets us a refill on our coffee, I would like to suggest that for the time being we just spend the next few weeks sharing more deeply than we have these last few weeks. By then we can find out what it is that we want to be as a group. In the meantime, let's agree that we will continue to meet here at Barbara's house each Thursday morning from 10:00 to 11:30.

Sally: The sharing group idea is fine with me, but Jane suggested we study the Bible, and maybe someone else feels this same need. Could we be a sharing group for the next few weeks, but also ask different ones to begin with a short devotional each time?

Lynn: I would like to suggest that the devotional time not be more than five minutes, though, so we will have most of the time to spend on sharing, at least for the next few weeks.

Jane: I want to be part of the group, but I don't know if I can share like I hear some of you talking about. I was raised never to share feelings, and it is very difficult for me to do this. Where I grew up, a person's business was his own, and no one meddled in it. But, I need to talk about some of these same things that we've been talking about here today. I just don't know if I can.

This group agreed that no one *had* to share, but there had emerged a consensus, without its being imposed on anyone, that the group, for a while, at least, would be a sharing group. To be a sharing group simply implied that they were willing to struggle with the two essential questions of any group that goes through the initial phase of group growth: (1) Can we risk being honest and trusting? (2) What is our purpose? Until consensus emerges about these two questions so that relationships can move to be experienced at a deeper level, and purpose centers around a definite group consensus, the sharing group remains at a superficial level of risk and purpose.

This group had taken the first steps in the answer to both of these essential questions. They had agreed that they were willing to struggle in a climate of honesty and caring for each other, and that their purpose would be to become a sharing group centered around personal spiritual growth.

Groups in the life of the church do go through stages which are similar from group to group. If the persons above had decided just to remain a Thursday morning coffee group, this would have determined the level of involvement with each other, and would have determined a particular direction of purpose. But, somewhere along the way some may have wondered why the sharing had never gone very deep and seemed to always remain superficial; and why projects brought up in the group were only thought of as "good ideas," and "someone should do something about that!"

But, the group had decided to risk relationships at a deeper level which would produce some agony, but would also be the kind of climate in which God could give his gift of fellowship (*koinonia*). They had decided on a purpose, which, though they were not aware of it at that time, was really a purpose to be a personal spiritual growth sharing group. As the group would evolve, soon just meeting to share would not be enough. One of the important principles of group development which persons need to constantly be aware of is the principle of evolvement. We must expect that where God calls us today is not where he may call us tomorrow; and where he calls us tomorrow may not be where he will call us the next day. Our response tends to be just for today, and we want to fix it; firm it up; and nail it down, saying once and for all, "God, I responded!" But, God's question to us is, "Did you respond to today's call?" The Gospel writer records Jesus as saying, "Take up your cross *daily* and follow me" (Luke 9:23).

There would be other issues that the group would have to deal with in future sessions, but the development of that day had been real and effective to the point of that day's needs. Each time the group would meet the question of how much could be risked at different levels and still be accepted by the group members, would emerge in new forms. Also, they would continue to deal with how much could be trusted with the other group members without it being spread all over the church and community. Finally, they would have to come to that point where they would have to deal with the other issues which had been brought up in the group that day, but which had not been dealt with in terms of a group concensus. There would be questions of group leadership: who was going to lead each time, and was leadership to be shared or would the leader be just one person? How were group members going to support each other during the week when one of the group members needed another person in a time of need? And, how would the wives share with their husbands what was going on and the new growth that was being experienced in their own lives?

Many of these and other questions would come to a resolution in the form of group-discovered and group-imposed disciplines by which the, now struggling, community would order its life. And, they would probably come out at about the same point that many other groups have discovered over the past few years. They would discover the need to have some minimum form of group discipline which might include such elements as:

(1) weekly attendance, unless providentially hindered;
(2) some form of daily study of the Scriptures, or a common book being used by the group;
(3) daily time of prayer for each member; and
(4) confidentiality of that which was shared in the group.

8 Understanding the Dynamics of Small Groups

Well, there you sat in the first group meeting. You rubbed your hands together; you crossed and uncrossed your legs; you cleared your throat; and you wondered what everyone else was thinking. You were looking at everyone and they all were seemingly looking at you. Finally, someone spoke. You felt like hugging them. But, the silence was broken only for a moment and you were on your way again wondering what this was all about. Pretty soon you quit rubbing your hands and crossing and uncrossing your legs. The group had really begun this time as persons began to share and you were right in the middle of it. That was great! But, were you aware of the dynamics; the said and unsaid things around you?

Look and Listen

Group dynamics is a term to describe something that is constantly taking place in the group. Because of these "dynamics, the group is always moving, changing, interacting, and reacting, The direction any group takes is dependent upon the forces exerted on it both from within and without." [1]

Group dynamics is not something you have or have not. Group dynamics are. Every group has dynamics. The importance of understanding these dynamics cannot be overstated. A good rule of thumb is, "When informed attention is paid to group processes, the chances increase that a group will be able to reach maturity and fulfill its potentiality." [2] The other side of that same coin is the fact that if a group or individual ignores the dynamic processes, those same dynamics may bring about failure.

Therefore, when we are talking about the dynamics of a group, remember that both *content* and *process* are important in the group. Both deserve attention. Those who focus only on the content and fail to appreciate the process of interaction will miss a great deal of what is taking place in the group. So look at your group. Look and listen! Something is probably happening that you need to see and hear.

A point to always remember is that communication is always taking place in a group. Some of it is verbal, much of it is nonverbal. Therefore, if you depend only upon your ears for knowing what is going on you will miss much of what is really taking place.

It is a fact that we communicate a lot with our bodies, our faces, our hands, our legs, our feet. Interest or boredom will be evident depending upon the use of the body in communicating.

Look around you in your group. Look at what the others are doing with their hands and feet. Look at their faces, their eyes. What feelings do you get as you look? Do they look interested or bored or tired? Listening with your eyes demands that you pay attention to what is taking place in the group.

Yesterday I was in the office of a man; and as we sat and talked, I began to get a feeling that he wasn't really with me. He had his arms on the arms of the chair and seemed to be lifting his body up and out of the chair. He appeared tense, and focused his eyes elsewhere. This bothered me. Here I was at his invitation. Over the telephone he had sounded excited about our time together. But now, his questions weren't sharp, his interest lacked something, and his body was saying let's get this over with. I knew he wasn't really listening to me. Finally, I placed some materials on his desk and excused myself. As I did this, he turned to me and said, "I feel that I ought to tell you something. I am uneasy today. I have a close friend whose wife is dying. I am supposed to sit with her tonight at the hospital. I am hurting for the family." After a few more words we agreed to get together again, then I left.

There is always what some call the "hidden agenda" in all of our lives. It involves the things that have affected us that day, the things we left undone; in fact, our entire past walks into that room in a way that many times we are unconscious of. People cannot walk into a meeting and just leave all of their problems, feelings, and emotions outside the door. They bring them with them. If the problem is very big, then it will interfere with communication. Recognizing this is very important. There is an old saying, "Don't believe everything you hear and only half of what you see." This really fits the group situation. There are many times in a group when you can be "listening" with all of your might and still not "hear what the person has said." Remember that persons rarely say what they are meaning or feeling. So you need to learn to be able to hear what they are saying or not saying.

Carlyle Marney, the founder and director of Interpreters' House, calls his conferences for ministers "a school of hearing." Marney has enabled many ministers to be able to hear what a person has said, or thinks he said, or said, but didn't mean. According to Marney, the listener has a big responsibility to the speaker and to himself. It is the listener who should say, "I heard you saying this," or "Are you saying thus and so?" or "Is this what you mean?" Only one, then, who is listening can be the "interpreter" or "clarifier." He has the unique privilege of helping the speaker and himself to understand. The speaker, on the other hand, can also help the listener. He may say, "Yes, that is what I said," or "No, that is not what I said," Or "Yes, that is what I said, but I didn't mean just that." Or, he may say, "No that is not what I said, but it is closer to what I am feeling."

Learning to listen is so important to the welfare of a group. Interpretation and clarification can really enhance communication of the group. Not only does every person have the right to speak, they also have the right to be heard.

Thus, dynamics, content plus process, are the forces which operate to hold a group together, or cause it to fail. Dynamics can be positive, negative, or neutral. Reid says:

When they are positive and people in a group seem to be getting along happily and productively, there is little need to be concerned about the dynamics of the situation. However, when the interaction between group members is negative and unproductive, or even neutral and lukewarm, we need to know what processes are blocking communication.[3]

Some of the matters to be looked for in the dynamics of a group are: (1) *The group climate*—is it hostile, uncomfortable, warm, or cool. (2) *Patterns of participation*—is everyone talking, no one talking, one person dominating the conversation, who speaks to whom, and what are the patterns of conversation. (3) *Flight and engagement*—the avoidance of a "touchy" issue is flight, or it may be the decision to not engage in that unpleasant issue at this point, while engagement is taking hold of an issue, even if it is uncomfortable. (4) *Leadership competition*—in a group where there is no designated leader, only a convenor, there may emerge out of hidden agendas in each person, a struggle for leadership which can become a struggle for identity—when leadership is shared, however, a willingness to follow on behalf of the rest of the group must be demonstrated so that leadership roles are not constantly challenged. (5) *Hidden agenda*—again, is that which we bring into any meeting which affects our personal, and therefore, the group's behavior. (6) *Timing*—sometimes ideas are great, but the timing of their presentation is off and the group rejects or does not respond to them. (7) *Trust level*—has to do with "Are we still playing games with each other?" or has there been a lowering of our masks. This depends on the climate of trust that a group has developed.[4]

Thus, the dynamics of a group, what is seen and heard, plus an awareness of what lies below the surface, helps a group to "feel" what is going on in a group. How does the group feel—ask this to several persons in a group (not just one, because the hidden agenda of that person's day may be misleading to the group feeling) and you may begin to get an idea of what is the group climate.

Group Member Roles

"Another aspect of group life that is crucial in understanding a group's behavior, diagnosing its problems, and improving its operation, is the way in which various required functions are performed." [5] One of the most widely recognized classification of these functions are (1) group-building and maintenance roles, which help build cohesiveness and relationships, and (2) group task roles, which help guide the group towards its goal.

Building and Maintenance Roles

Encourager—this person demonstrates by words and actions that he welcomes and appreciates the presence and input of the others.

Harmonizer—opens people up to exploring new ideas; he reconciles differences and reduces tension.

Gate Keeper—helps to keep the conversation open and flowing; encourages others to get involved in the discussion.

Standard Setter—sets the standards for the group to achieve.

Follower—is willing to go along with the group; this person compromises in order to keep group unity.

Task Roles

Imitator-Contributor—proposes tasks or goals; defines the groups' problems; suggests methods or procedures for solving the problems.

Information Seeker—requests facts or opinions; seeks out ideas or suggestions from the other group members.

Information Giver—offers facts or opinions; provides the group with relevant information.

Coordinator—helps bring the information together; clarifies; defines terms; offers alternative suggestions.

Orientor—helps to set things straight; to bring things together so the group will stay on the proper course.

Evaluator—offers a decision or conclusion to what has been said in the group; weighs the information received and offers an opinion.[6]

All persons are more comfortable in one role than in another. Check yourself out after you have been involved in a group. Ask yourself, What role did I play most often? The possibility is that this is the role you play in all groups. Just remember, you are an important member to the group. The role that you play may very well be the strength that the group needs.

There are also some "nonfunctional" roles that some members often play. Basically these meet no need in the group itself, and they actually hinder the group from reaching its goals. They need to be recognized here because of their negative influence on the group. These nonfunctional roles are:

Blocker—puts obstacles in the path of the group; restricts the movement of the group by interfering with group process.

Dominator—wants to command the group; wants to be the

guiding force behind all that happens; tries to control all that
goes on in the group.

Recognition Seeker—desires to have all of the credit for any
gains achieved; insists on being recognized as the one who made
it all happen; has to be at the center of attention.

Aggressor—attacks others; criticizes other members; openly
displays hostility that has no relationship to the group.

Avoider—shuns the group; withdraws from the discussion and
decision-making process.[7]

The participation of these people in a group can be a detriment.
A group that understands the dynamics and learns to recognize
these persons can, by taking the right action, preserve the life
of the group and help these persons recognize their negative roles.

Games People Play in Groups

There are also persons in some groups who seem to play "games"
as a defense in groups as a way to keep from being real and
authentic. These games have to be dealt with by any group so
as to help the dynamics of the group move off of these "dead
centers," help the person become aware of the game they are
playing, and lead the group back into more productive channels
of work according to the sharing group's purpose.

Hysterical Al: Al carries with him his own personal "wailing
wall"; he cries at everything he shares. Everything upsets him.
He is also an alarmist; he is alarmed over everything that is said.
He is a past master at making mountains out of molehills. Pretty
soon group members will watch what they say for fear of upsetting
Al.

Talkative Tom: Tom is all knowing, all thinking, and says all.
He has *the* answer to everyone's questions. He inflicts rather than
shares. Others in the group would have said something two meetings ago, but they don't know how to interrupt Tom. Pretty soon
the other group members feel that what they have to say is not
important, or at least they feel that Tom wouldn't hear them.

Helpful Helen: Here is the group's "mother." Helen will help
anyone out, whether they want it or not. She always "knows"
how you feel, what you "intended" to say, and what you didn't
mean to say. She also knows what you should do about whatever

is bothering you. Helen is playing another game also. If she helps you when you "need" help, then surely you will come to her rescue when she is in a tight spot. Helen doesn't allow anyone to walk by themselves. She holds hands; smooths over difficult questions; and tries not to allow any negative sharing to emerge.

Naive Nel: Nel never heard of the doubts and questions people raise. She is simply aghast at whatever persons share honestly. That people could feel, much less say those things, is news to her. If the group confronts Nel too forcefully about this, it may destroy her protective world view and maybe do more harm than good.

Prosecuting Dan: He has been in groups before and knows how to "open" people up. He represents a one-man attack force. His motto is, "break them down and they will get real." He disables people with a barrage of questions, to which he also supplies the answers. Dan is simply brutal with members of the group. His defense is, "I am only trying to help." But, really this is a protective shell to keep others from getting too close to him.

Psychiatrist Rick: Rick displays an awesome astuteness for psychoanalyzing everyone. He misses nothing. He feels the need to analyze every word and every movement. Rick hasn't come to the place yet where a person crosses his legs just to get into a more comfortable position. For him, it has a subconscious motive, which he seeks. Rick often misses the obvious while searching for the hidden. He paralyzes as he analyzes.

Try-Harder Rose: Rose defies all help. The group cannot really help her. She has tried all of their suggestions and found them worthless. Nevertheless, she succeeds in getting the group focused on her and her needs, getting them to try harder each time.

Quiet Quinn: Quinn encourages everyone to talk, to "share" themselves. Meanwhile he never reveals anything. Exposure is fine for the other members. Quinn isn't going to risk anything.

Group Guidelines—The Group Contract

Leslie points out that in groups that do not use professional leaders there is a greater need for group guidelines, sometimes called the group's contract.[8] Guidelines are not rules. They are merely suggestions for enabling the group process. They are intended in no way to limit the dynamics of the group. Nevertheless, it is necessary that all of the members agree to the guidelines, which each group develops. They form part of the basic group "contract."

The word "contract" simply means that a group has decided through consensus what to do. In other terms, it may be called group disciplines. When a group first meets, the question should be asked around the circle of members, "Why did you come, and what do you hope to get out of such a sharing group as this?" This question asked at the first meeting of the group, towards the close of the meeting, will give each person a chance to express his/her feelings about the purpose of the group and to hear each other person express his/her idea about the purpose.

Later in the group's life, when there is a need to arrive at a common purpose for the remaining weeks of a group's existence, these statements will be amplified to state a more lasting group purpose. The more specific a group's contract, or guidelines, or disciplines, can be developed, the more successful the group will be.

The first meeting when each individual states his reason for being there, the reasons should be heard, but no one should be held to those purposes. The contract will *evolve* as the group continues to build relationships and a new level of trust and risk emerge. Thus, a contract can evolve, and should be expected to from the first night to about the fifth week, when a group has to really grapple with its on-going purpose. The following list gives some possible areas of a group's contract with each other. Remember, a contract among group members is specific, and it has to be one that is arrived at by the entire group members who are willing to commit themselves to it for a specific time. It says something definite about the purpose of the group meeting week after week, a purpose that each person is willing to commit himself to for a specific period of time. And contracts evolve as the group, by consensus, sees its purpose change.

1. Be on time for all group meetings.
2. End the meeting on time.
3. Stay for the entire meeting.
4. No one person should dominate the conversation; everyone

should be given an opportunity to speak.

5. The discussion should be kept on the right track. Chasing rabbits is fine if you are after rabbits.

6. There should be no whispering in the group. If someone has something to say, it should be said to the entire group.

7. Absences must be kept to a minumum.

8. The group is bound by confidentiality. What is said in the group remains there.

9. Listen to what is being said. If you don't understand something, say so. You owe it to yourself and to the group to be clear on all points.

10. There are no spectators in the group, only participants.

11. The focus is on affirming people, not on destroying them.

12. Don't leave a person hanging at the end of a session. Allow time to clear up any agenda items.

13. Be flexible, even with your guidelines.

There is no doubt that other guidelines can be added to this list. Perhaps your groups will choose to do so. However, these do offer a starting point.

Stages of Group Development

Every group goes through some stages before they really become a working group. Bion has given us a list of stages which I feel can be applied to almost any group.[9]

Ambiguity—at this stage personal feelings are more prevalent than the work to be done. Differences of opinion are evident among the group members. These personal feelings influence group behavior.

Revolt—revolt can occur easily during the period of ambiguity. Generally, it may be against the convenor; however, members can revolt against one another also. The issue may well revolve around each person's preconceived idea of what is supposed to happen in a group.

Work—this, as a rule, follows the revolt. This not only puts the group on the right track, but does much toward releasing the tension built up by the revolt.

Consensus—this follows the work stage. Without any detailed plan the group just seems to come together to work.

Consolidation—this is the attitude of "win some, lose some." This is the stage at which the group counts their gains, evaluates their losses, and unites around their common goals.

Conclusion

A gathering of eight to twelve people does not constitute a group. A true group consists of a certain number of people who have committed themselves to one another and to a common goal. In essence they have agreed to struggle together. They have pledged to become vunerable to one another, and to care for one another.

Bill Cusak has pointed out four freedoms that are basic to such a group.[10] They are:

1. *The freedom to trust.* This gives us freedom from fear. I am free to trust you when I turn away from the fear of being found out by you.

2. *The freedom to be one.* I don't have to make it by myself, indeed I can't. This freedom means that I can be one with you through Christ. Oneness comes as a group reaches community.

3. *The freedom to lead.* The leadership of the group should be shared. You will need to do your part. No one person is competent enough to see and understand all of the dynamics of a meeting.

4. *The freedom to fail.* Most of us don't allow ourselves this freedom. Too often I only have the freedom to succeed, never to fail. Not having this freedom places a tremendous responsibility and burden on one's shoulders, a responsibility and burden that no one should have to carry. Allow yourself this freedom.

Small groups have been very meaningful to me. I hope that as you participate in your own group you will find your niche, your place, your ministry. A small group can be a joy, an oasis, a party, a place of refuge, a place of healing. Much can happen when committed people get together and really care for one another.

Notes

1. Malcolm and Hulda Knowles, *Introduction to Group Dynamics* (New York: Association Press, 1959), p. 12.

2. Clyde Reid, *Groups Alive—Church Alive* (New York: Harper & Row, 1969), p. 47.

   3. *Ibid.*, pp. 46-47.
   4. *Ibid.*, pp. 48-56.
   5. Knowles, *op. cit.*, pp. 51-52.
   6. *Ibid.*, pp. 52-54.
   7. *Ibid.*, pp. 54-55.
   8. Leslie, *op. cit.*, p. 138.
   9. W. R. Bion, *Experiences in Groups* (New York: Basic Books, 1961).
   10. John Hendrix, ed., *On Becoming a Group* (Nashville: Broadman Press), pp. 78-79.

9 Support for Mission—"AMBEK"

A mission group, in the Broadmoore Baptist Church, was formed after the observance of the church's annual Race Relations Sunday. One person in the church was asking the church leadership: "What do we do now? Is this all we do to better relationships between black and white Baptist churches?"

The pastor and minister of education, wanting to encourage the formation of mission groups, where persons could receive the mutual support and care needed for genuine involvement in community and mission, encouraged Ruth Murphy to "sound the call to mission." She told them that the call to mission she was feeling seemed to be at the point of building closer bonds of fellowship between black and white Baptist churches. She said she felt that the time of rhetoric was over, when all people did was nothing more than simply say, "They are our brothers." She said the question that kept bothering her was, When are we going to move beyond words to doing something about making this a reality?

She pointed out that most black Baptists lived in one area of town, where most of their churches were also located, while white Baptists lived in another part of town with their churches. She said: "What we've got is two ghettos; one white and one black. How can we build fellowship when we never see each other? What I would like to see done," she continued, "is to see us make attempts at finding ways to build fellowship between the white and black Baptist churches, so at least we could have one Baptist fellowship in this town and stop the perpetuating of Sunday being the most segregated day of the week."

"Fine, Ruth," answered Bob Adams, the pastor, "but how do you want to go about that?"

"I don't know," she said, "so I've come to you for some ideas."

113

That was when the two men suggested the formation of a mission group built around persons who felt this same call to mission. They knew that over the past year and a half ten sharing groups had been in existence in the church and many persons had come to the point of discovering their own gifts for mission. They also were aware that this same point of mission had been raised by some other persons in the sharing groups, but, as yet, no one had been willing to stand up and call the others to this particular mission. Now here was the person, who might be the one to issue the call to a mission of race relations that these others, who shared this concern for mission from the sharing groups, might hear and respond to. So they encouraged Ruth to issue the "call to mission of building fellowship between black and white Baptist churches" from the pulpit during the next Sunday's morning worship service. This was a new experience for the church, its leadership, and for Ruth, but nine persons responded.

A year has passed since that initial call to mission and the group has been meeting weekly on Sunday evenings since. During this first year most of the time had been spent in forming a deeper sense of community, defining and redefining the call to mission of the group, calling out the gifts of leadership in the group, working on the disciplines of spiritual formation and accountability of each of the group members, and a study of the roots of racial problems between blacks and whites, especially among Baptists.

Their actual successes in mission accomplishment had been few thus far. They had sponsored a more meaningful Race Relations Sunday observance the following year in which their church had had a chance to know firsthand the black worship experience with choir and preacher from the black church being at Broadmoore. Beyond that they were in the process of exploring some small fellowship groups between the two Baptist churches; they had formed a joint committee between the two Baptist bodies in the town to explore other areas of need between blacks and whites; and they had discovered some of the difficult economic and political problems of what it means to live as a minority people.

It was at this point that the mission group was beginning to have its first agony of mission, for some members were still only committed to creating fellowship groups among black and white Baptists, while some of the members had begun to point to the need of the mission group to grapple with the economic and political structures that continued to keep minority people in their oppression in such areas as adequate housing, equal job opportunities, equal education, and a fair political voice in governing their own affairs.

The *activist*, or group mission facilitator, had been exploring ways to become involved in a ministry to the "brokenness" of these four areas and two of the mission group members had already taken their realtors' exam as a means for selling houses in all-white subdivisions to blacks through a black real estate company. This had been done, not without a little pain and confrontation with the town's economic and political structures. The first house they tried to sell ended up in a federal court suit against the builder, who tried to say his house wasn't available when he found out the customer was a black family. The second and third houses were in subdivisions where some of the other church members lived, and hostile phone calls and even some threats of retaliation had come.

But, the mission group provided both a place for healing these wounds and a place for holding Ruth and Julie accountable for the exercising of their gifts for mission in selling houses even during those first few bitter, painful days. The mission group helped those members "learn to live" with the "agony" of sustained mission at the point of confrontation between God's will of reconciliation to wholeness and healing and the world's will (even expressed through some well-meaning church members) to death.

The name the mission group had chosen was AMBEK from the biblical question, "Am I my brother's keeper?" They were, in their call to this mission of bringing healing to the brokenness between the two races, answering, "Yes!" The group met once a week for two hours of worship, study, and sharing, and then each member was involved another day or two during the week in some aspect of the group's mission.

Two weeks into the second year and just after the group's annual recommitment to the mission, the twelve persons (nine from the original core group, and three who had just joined the group for a period of "associate membership" until they decided on whether to make the full commitment to the disciplined life of the group) silently came into the meeting room after the evening worship service which had taken place between 5:15-6:15 P.M. They took their seats in the chairs, which had been arranged in a circle and began the group time of worship which lasted for the first thirty minutes of each meeting.

Each week a different person took responsibility for selecting the Scripture readings, the meditative thought and leading the group in the song. The worship had come to be an important experience of "centering down" by each member as they came in from a busy world. Also, this type of worship experience made each person both a participant and a leader. The group used the following schedule:

1. Devotions begin with *10 minutes of silence.* Come in and be seated, and in silence seek to be collected; to be centered in your own being in such a way you can hear the still, small voice instruct you for this day.

2. The silence will be broken by the *singing of a song,* followed by a reading from the *Gospels,* a reading from the *Letters,* and a brief *meditative thought.*

3. Following comes a time of silence which can be used as the Spirit leads: (1) to listen to others share from thoughts or experiences they have—*please break the silence and share whatever the Spirit leads you to say*—or (2) simply to sit and meditate on the readings of the devotional period and the meditative thoughts.

4. The devotional period will be concluded with the *singing of a song.*

The worship had begun with ten minutes of silence. Persons came into the room in one's and two's, were seated, and in silence sought to be a collected person in such a way that each could hear the "still, small voice" instruct them for their meeting together.

After ten minutes, the silence was broken by Fran, who with her clear alto voice, started singing "God Is So Good," followed by a second verse of the same, simple melody, "He Never Fails."

After a brief moment of silence, Harold read from the Gospels the passage found in John 15:1-11 about the relationship of the vine to the branches, used by Jesus to show the relationship of the disciple to his Lord. Another brief pause of silence was followed by a reading from Paul's letters to the churches. This time the passage was from Galatians 5:22-26, read by Connie, the only teenager in the group. Finally, another pause and Fran, who had been designated the worship leader for this week, read the following meditative thought from one of Thomas Merton's books:

Real Christian living is *stunted* and *frustrated* if it remains content with the bare externals of worship, with "saying prayers" and "going to church," with fulfilling one's external duties and merely being respectable. The real purpose of prayer (in the fully personal sense as well as in the Christian assembly) is the deepening of personal realization in love, the awareness of God (even if sometimes this awareness may amount to a negative factor, a seeming "absence"). The real purpose of meditation—or at least that which recommends itself as most relevant for modern man—is the exploration and discovery of new dimensions in freedom, illumination and love, in deepening our awareness of our life in Christ.

What is the relation of this to action? Simply this. He who attempts to act and do things for others or for the world without deepening his own self-understanding, freedom, integrity and capacity to love, will not have anything to give others. He will communicate to them nothing but the contagion of his own obsessions, his agressiveness, his ego-centered ambitions, his delusions about ends and means, his doctrinaire prejudices and ideas. There is nothing more tragic in the modern world than the misuse of power and action to which men are driven by their own Faustian misunderstandings and misapprehensions. We have more power at our disposal today than we have ever had, and yet we are more alienated and estranged from the inner ground of meaning and of love than we have ever been. The result of this is evident. We are living through the greatest crisis in the history of man; and this crisis is centered precisely in the country that has made a fetish out of action and has lost (or perhaps never had) the sense of contemplation. Far from being irrelevant, prayer, meditation and contemplation are of the utmost importance in America today. . . . Prayer and meditation have an important part to play in opening up new ways and new horizons. If our prayer is the expression of a deep and grace-inspired desire for newness of life—and not the mere blind attachment to what has always

been familiar and "safe"—God will act in us and through ūs to renew
the Church by preparing, in prayer, what we cannot yet imagine or
understand. In this way our prayer and faith today will be oriented
toward the future which we ourselves may never see fully realized on
earth.[1]

All of this had lasted less than twenty minutes and now, as
was their custom after the meditative selection, the group members
for the remaining ten minutes were free to share whatever the
Holy Spirit seemed to be leading them to add to or comment
on what had been read from the Scripture and the meditative
reading, or to remain in silence and meditate on the personal
meaning of those words. Sometimes there were deep and meaningful sharings by one or several persons. This night, however, the
group seemed to just want to use the time for meditation.

Finally, thirty minutes after the worship experience had begun,
Fran again led out in the singing of "Amazing Grace" and the
group ended the first part of its meeting which had begun with
a time of worship. It was this way each week as they met, and
the group had found, no matter how pressing the mission task
was, or the pressure of time to get on with the business of mission,
they could not do the work of the group if they didn't begin
with this time of worship, made up of silence, song, Scripture
readings, reading from a devotional classic, and personal devotional sharings.

The study that night was being led by Steve, who in business
life was a mortician at a local funeral home. Steve's "gift" had
been affirmed by the group as the person who stayed in touch
with what was happening at city hall and in the county government. Because of the kind of work he was in, he had available
time to "monitor" the political systems of local government and
knew what was, and was not, being done in the various economic
and political arenas, and who had to be seen when something
needed to be done.

When the group was looking for its study area for the next
three months, Steve had suggested it might help if the group
was able to identify the economic and political structures of
society, especially those in their county and city, which held blacks
in oppression and did not allow them to be free. So, for two

weeks the study had been going on under the leadership of the head of the Community Action Council of one of the neighborhoods where blacks lived.

It was not unusual for the mission group to get an "expert" in some particular area of study to do the initial exploration of an area of study. Yet, in no way did this imply that only "experts" could minister in a meaningful way. Already, this mission group was becoming, through their study, community life, and mission involvement, more expert in building bridges of understanding and ministry than some of the government-sponsored organizations, who had in recent weeks come to the AMBEK group for "advice." But, this night was the third session in exploring this new area of the political structures of the community and the way political power was used to exploit people.

The study presentation was made by the CAC representative for thirty minutes, followed by a twenty-minute dialogue.

Finally, the last forty minutes of the weekly meeting were spent in sharing by group members. There was talk of how different persons had had difficulty in keeping particular disciplines during the week; ways in which God had addressed them through the Scriptures during the week; crucial problems that were being faced, both personally and in different areas of the corporate mission; and particular joys of affirmation that had come during the week as a result of God's activity in their lives. Each one, conscious of the time, kept their remarks brief in order not to monopolize the time and to give others time to share.

Also, as a means of accountability in personal Christian growth and responsibility to the community, it was agreed that one person each week, in addition to weekly written reports to their own personal spiritual growth director, would present to the total group some excerpts from his weekly report which would give the group an idea of each person's progress in spiritual growth. This week it was Ruth's turn.

Ruth was one of the two women who had taken their realtor's exam in order to minister to black families who were looking for adequate housing in what had been all-white, middle-income subdivisions. Their confrontation of housing problems and of the economic structures had caused a great deal of pain to Ruth and

Julie which the group had had to minister to time and again as both women had had to deal with their own feelings of hatred, resentment and despair. They had encountered loan companies that would not loan money to blacks to buy in white subdivisions; had experienced political pressures brought to revoke their licenses; and attempts to get around existing laws which guaranteed both equal housing opportunities and stiff penalties for failure to meet those codes. But, time and again the mission group had been *both* a source of accountability for continuing to exercise their gifts of mission, and a means for healing their wounds of confrontation.

This session Ruth began her spiritual report with the words, "I have been having difficulty the last two weeks with my daily devotional time. It seems the more I am aware of the many needs in improving race relations and seek to be involved more, the greater the difficulty I am having in maintaining the hour of daily Scripture meditation, prayer, and silence. My mind just simply refuses to focus on what I am doing; it wanders off on all the things I need to be doing. So, I've let my quiet time slip for the past several weeks. Oh, I've done it about three days out of seven, but I've not met the minimum discipline of living daily with the Scriptures and a daily time of prayer."

Fran, who served as the group's spiritual growth director, asked Ruth, "Have you noticed any difference in the quality of the work you've been doing?"

"No," replied Ruth. "But, I do know that I am beginning to tire from doing some of the things I'm doing."

"Such as?"

"Well, it is beginning to irritate me at times, not all the time, but at times, to have to take so many people to see houses who are just shopping. They really aren't interested in buying; in fact, many of them couldn't borrow the money if they had to. So, I feel like they are just taking up my time, which I could better spend with those black families who are seriously searching for adequate housing."

The discussion among the other group members continued for about twenty more minutes about this difficulty Ruth was facing and how this irritation with people needed to be explored more fully, for there could be emerging another aspect of ministry that Ruth had not been aware of in her original call to sell houses. This need to explore the involvement of her call was urged on Ruth as well as a need to return to her daily Scripture readings and time of prayer, meditation, and contemplation. Her own personal spiritual growth director, who in this case was her co-laborer in real estate, Julie, was urged to work with Ruth on the two areas.

The group meeting closed in different ways each time. This time, Carl, who served as the one to help persons in calling out their gifts for ministry, suggested that the group stand up and form a circle with Ruth standing in the middle. Then, each person in the group of twelve would in one word give a gift of affirmation to Ruth; something that she could use in growing in both her inward journey and her outward mission. One by one the words started coming: patience, endurance, discernment . . . .

NOTES

1. Merton, *Contemplation in a World of Action*, pp. 178-79.

10 Mission Groups—Growth in Mission

Jesus stood in the synagogue of Nazareth on the day of worship and announced his mission in these words:

The spirit of the Lord is upon me, because he has annointed me to preach good news to the poor. He has sent me to proclaim release to the captives and recovering of sight to the blind, to set at liberty those who are oppressed, to proclaim the acceptable year of the Lord (Luke 4:18-19, RSV).

True, these words which Jesus read that day had been written hundreds of years before by the prophet Isaiah (61:1-2); but Jesus' words, "Today this scripture has been fulfilled in your hearing," indicated, according to Luke's narrative, that Jesus had taken those words literally to be the essence of his mission here on earth.

The mission that Jesus announced to those in that place of worship that day were not taken by the hearers any more seriously than Israel had taken them seriously at various points in her previous history. The failure to fulfill God's original mission for Israel ultimately led to Jesus' lament during one of his visits to Jerusalem in words that symbolized the failure of Israel to be a leaven people among the nations, "Would that even today you knew the things that make for peace! But now they are hid from your eyes" (Luke 19:42). During another visit, maybe his last, to the city, he indicated the inseparable cleavage that had caused this final condemnation of the city that David loved:

O Jerusalem, Jerusalem, killing the prophets and stoning those who are sent to you! How often would I have gathered your children together as a hen gathers her brood under her wings, and you would not! Behold your house is forsaken. And I tell you, you will not see me until you say, "Blessed is he who comes in the name of the Lord!" (Luke 13:34-35).

The failure to fulfill the mission by the nation Israel that God had intended from the beginning, and one preached by God's messengers throughout the Scriptures, is what Jesus came to restore. And her rejection of that mission by killing the Son, who had been sent to call the nation back to the mission, resulted in the calling out of a new Israel, whom Paul called a new graft to the old tree: "They [Israel] were broken off because of their unbelief, but you stand fast only through faith. So do not become proud, but stand in awe. For if God did not spare the natural branches, neither will he spare you" (Rom. 11:20-21).

Thus, the purpose of God's people, his church (the called out ones), and consequently the ultimate purpose of small groups, is *not* to end up turned in on themselves, but to be engaged with God in mission. As Gordon Cosby has said, if small groups just meet to be meeting and enjoying the fellowship of a warm intimate community *alone,* the small group will continue to turn more and more inward, protecting itself, but at the same time "destroying its pilgrims." [1] The "journey inward" that had been begun in the sharing groups must come to grips with the new dimension of the "journey outward" if there is to be real power and endurance to small groups in the church. Otherwise, they become just another fad, which the church has tasted and once gotten all the juice out of, like chewing gum, is discarded in the endless search for the next fad, and the next fad, and so on.

The call to mission, both individually and corporately, is basic to the life of the church, as is *koinonia,* and must be seriously examined and undertaken. Small groups in the evolvement of their life eventually come to that juncture where, in the examination of the journey into self, others, and God have to come face to face with the question, "So what?" What does all of this have to do with me and the vitality of the life of the church?

It is at this point that sharing groups need to be led into the deeper dimensions of mission groups where the two questions of (1) life lived out of deep community, and (2) life lived in a deep involvement in Christ's mission of reconciliation to that brokenness can be fully explored. This is the point of deeper commitment that most of us avoid. Meister Eckhart is quoted as having said: "There are plenty to follow our Lord half-way, but not the other half. They will give up possession, friends, and

honors; but it touches them too closely to disown themselves." [2]
This is the question of mission groups. Sharing groups have given
us a taste of what it is to grow in fellowship and personal growth,
but these are really to no avail if they are not followed by growth
in mission. This is also more costly growth for it involves becoming
a corporate group (which involves giving up more of self in order
to be), and a living out of life at the point of encounter where
the will of the world intersects the will of God—the point where
brokenness is seen and heard and the point where healing and
freedom need to be offered.

To hold in creative tension the two dimensions of being both
an inward person, who is in touch with self and in daily conversation with God through prayer and a study of the Scriptures,
and at the same time an outward person, where one is engaged
in the ministry and witness of the good news to brokenness, is
the multidimensional approach of mission support groups.

There are many persons who would like to be just an inward
person, and many more, in their activism to change the world,
would like to be only an outward person. But, the demand of
God is that we be both. Cosby says that the inward and the outward
dimensions are but two sides of the same coin. Those who are
only inward must learn to be outward; and those who are activists
must learn to cultivate their inward dimensions. He said:

If the two are not together, a person becomes power-less and the
quality of their activity is nothing more than the quality of activity
of the world's activity. The work of the church must be different in
the quality of its social action, its mission, than other groups, who maybe
are doing the same thing. When you come up against the systems of
society (which are really worse than you think they are) you pretty
soon become aware of the power of the demonic. So, what we believe
is that, if anything is going to be done, it is going to happen by the
power of God's Holy Spirit. Therefore, we have to learn to channel
that power to heal and make new, and we can't do this unless we
are on this inward journey, and living out lives at that juncture point
in life where the Will of the World (which is to death as suicide) meets
the Will of God (which is to life, wholeness, freedom and fulfillment).
There we bring to bear another quality of life as we are the channels
of the power of the Holy Spirit.

Mission groups seek to hold both dimensions in a dynamic, creative tension in the lives of its members—a new dimension to individual and corporate Christianity that was explored and begun in sharing groups. As Thomas Kelly has so beautifully described this fullness of the Christian pilgrimage; it is a willingness "to be utterly obedient, to go the other half, to follow God's faintest whisper. But when such a commitment comes in a human life, God breaks through, miracles are wrought, world-renewing divine forces are released, history changes. There is nothing more important now than to have the human race endowed with just such committed lives." [3]

When mission groups emerge in the congregation, the best expression of church has been created. In mission groups both study and action have been combined into one unit. Both the individual nurture and growth of persons and the corporateness of mission involvement have come together. Both service and adoration, the original root meaning of the word worship, have taken on reality. But, just saying that mission groups can be the best expression of church does not resolve all the problems, especially for those who are committed to the fractured type of church life in which most congregations live today. Most church members live where study and service are never brought together; where individual personal Christian experience is never brought face to face with corporate Christian responsibility; where ministry and worship never interface. This is the problem with the fracturedness of much of local church Christianity today. The mission group seeks to bring these dimensions together within one unit and thus give new vitality to the worshiping, studying, and ministering congregational life.

The mission group is called to live out its life, individually and corporately, at the same point where Jesus was called to live out his mission. He has called us to this discipleship, and we are to bring the healing power of announcing this good news (the need to disciple) to those who despair, to bind up the wounds of those who hurt, to give sight to those who are blind, while setting free those who are held captive by whatever binds them. The church is in the business of reconciliation; of ministering to brokenness wherever it is found. That's what mission is all about, and that is the role of the mission group.

Mission groups supercede all other organizations in the life of the church except corporate congregational worship and corporate structures for serious study. Serious study is distinguished here from those study organizations in the church which are an end in themselves and do not lead to other areas of serious commitment to personal growth, community and mission. These organizations tend to consume their own product by existing only to get people to join them, attend regularly with no serious commitment beyond the meeting itself. In the mission group persons are confronted with all of the dimensions of personal and corporate growth (the journey into self, others, and God): individual and corporate accountability; individual and corporate worship (daily personal devotions and worship as a group); and individual and corporate ministry and witness. In the mission group, community can be experienced at its deepest dimensions, and the knowledge of one's self, gifts, and place of ministry are dealt within a structure of accountability for the exercising of those gifts for ministry and witness.

Beginning Mission Groups

How do mission groups begin, and when is the best time to make the transition from sharing groups to mission groups? What seems to be the appropriate time for this transition is that moment in which the members of the sharing group come to realize that the Christian life could be expressed in its entirety in the same dimensions that are being experienced in the small sharing group. That is, that caring, sharing, honesty, trust, openness, freedom, authenticity, growth, mission—all of these things that have been described as characteristics of the small sharing group—can be what church and the personal Christian life is all about. Sometimes I have described this point of transition as that thing that happens in the comic strips when the comic strip character sees the light bulb turn on. In psychological terms it is called "insight"; that moment when all of a sudden you see the solution, or the glimpse of the totality of what could be.

I believe that moment of "breakthrough" is precisely the time in which the possibility and the concept of the continuing mission

group should be presented. This will take sensitivity and a continual relatedness on the part of the pastor, or other church leadership, to know when that moment has occurred in a group. But,
it is precisely at *that moment* that the step into the mission group
should be presented with all of its rewards and costs. This can
be done on a weekend retreat or during an extended weekly session
of the regular sharing group's meeting. But, this is that crucial
point in the development of the group's life that must be ministered to if groups are to move out beyond the simple sharing
process.

In presenting the concept of the mission group, church leadership should not expect everyone to be a part of that kind of
group (nor should people be urged into one) for the depths of
community life, and the search for corporate mission, are costly
and persons should not be encouraged into them until they want
to be a part. The easiest and most costly error is to tell someone
to come into a mission group saying, "Try it out and see if you
won't like it." The mission group, though this may sound like
an elitist statement, has to be made up of a group of people
who "hunger" for community life, personal growth, and mission
involvement at deeper levels of their being. It cannot be a structure
that "everyone joins" in order to be accepted. There has to be
a hunger for this level of Christian living before a person seeks
to be a part of it.

If a person is not called to mission, and has not worked through,
at least to some degree, what it means to be the people of God
on mission, and has not grasped some idea of what his personal
gifts for ministry and witness are, then he should not be pushed
into a mission group.

Gordon Cosby defines a mission group this way: "It is a small
group of three to fifteen persons, conscious of the action of the
Holy Spirit in their lives, enabling them to hear the call of God
through Christ to belong in love to one another, and to offer
the gift of their corporate life for the world's healing and unity."
He goes on to say: "If a mission group has the capacity to continue
to hear the call of God, and to deal with its belongingness in
Christ, and to give its life in mission, it will of necessity be engaged
in an inward journey." He goes on to describe the minimal dimen-

sions of that inward journey; that is, what would be the basic disciplines from which the mission group can go on to develop its own disciplines. It will contain, according to Cosby, a group of people:

(1) who live under the Scripture.

(2) who will be deepening their life of prayer, which will include confession, meditation, and contemplation.

(3) who will be deepening their own self-understanding—a growing awareness of the "wounds" and blockages that keep us from adoration and the giving of ourselves, unreservedly, to one another—being in dialogue with one's self as the psalmist does.

(4) who will evoke the gifts of the Spirit in one another and the deepening of the corporate life that is given as gifts are exercised and responded to. The unity in the power of the group consists in the discovery of the gift of each member. If the church is to have power, every person who is called to join God in mission is given a gift of the Spirit and it is crucial that the mission group grapple with the gift of the Spirit so that everyone can understand and identify his gift. If you can't identify your gift, you can't grow in it. And, if you can't name your gift for mission, you can't be accountable for it. This means that the richness of the group is found in the multiplicity and variety of gifts in the group. It also means that as each person exercises his gift, the others are obedient to that gift. There emerges, therefore, in the group a mutuality of obedience to each other as well as authority over each other, thus, enabling the church to function with a supernatural power that has been promised to it.

(5) who will deal with the dimensions of personal and corporate worship.

(6) who will grapple with the issue of money and its management in order to be free enough to love in very practical ways within the community, both in terms of personal need within the group, and in terms of the resources available to accomplish mission on a sufficient enough scale to be demanding and exciting to people.

By its very nature, the mission group is also engaged on an "outward journey." Whereas most of the preceding elements deal with the "inward journey," the living out of the individual and corporate life at the juncture point of where the "Will of God" meets the "Will of the World," necessitates a "journey outward" into mission. Mission is a living out of both of these dimensions at that juncture point and whatever happens there happens. But, as an inward person and as an outward person, some ministry and witness therefore, can occur. Keeping these two dimensions in creative tension is very difficult, but necessary.

A mission group, therefore, comes into being in a very specific way. Cosby said, as they have tried to call mission groups into being in their own church, they tried several ways before finally finding that which seems to be a more satisfying approach. He said that he used to think that all you had to do was to:

Get a group of committed people together who would gather faithfully for Bible study and prayer, and the seeking of God's will for their lives and they would be then given a corporate mission. This did not happen. This is not a fruitful course to pursue, yet this is what almost every small group does. It gets together and says we are going to pray, and we are going to live under the Scriptures, and then we will be ready for this mission that God is going to give us. The only trouble with this is, it won't work because there is a great diversity of mission gifts in any group and the mission call heard by one person in the group is not the mission call of another. No *one* call to mission emerges in the group to which everyone can respond and so groups four or five years later are still looking for the mission.

Therefore, to attempt a common task fails because it did not take into account the deep inner responses of the Spirit of the other members of the group. You end up having to manipulate or maneuver the other members to get them to "hear" a mission call, for you've got all the other members of the group with their calls, and everybody can't get involved in mission at the same level if they are doing it at the point of call. They have come together on the wrong basis. [This is where mission groups differ from sharing groups.] The call that comes to be recognized by one person is not the call that has been recognized by another. No *one call* emerges in the group to which all in the group can respond.

Our procedure now is to start with one person, or a small nucleus of persons, who have heard a call for mission in one particular area, and let others gather around that call. Thus, the group begins with a clearly understood outward journey, and you don't have to wait two or three years down the road for the call to emerge. But, the group has also already achieved a clear commitment to an inward journey. It is crucial that these two dimensions be embodied from the very beginning of the group's life, otherwise, the group begins with many general hopes and aspirations and longings, but which remain just that for it is never able to agree on the common task to which it is called, or even the specifics of its disciplines.

The Calling Forth of Gifts
and the Call to Mission

Cosby says that in their church they have developed two essential elements of mission groups: the discovery of each individual's gifts for mission; and the necessity for a mission group to form around a particular call for mission. Thus, in their practice gift is used in two senses, though they have a common basis in the charisma, or the gift-bestowing power, of the Holy Spirit. Sharing groups, and even mission groups, continue a process of a discovery of a person's particular gifts for ministry and witness.

This search for personal gift for ministry and witness may last as long as several years and comes through the interaction of the group process and my own journey inward. It should culminate at a point where I have come to know my gifts for mission, either as an unused ability that I had but which had lain dormant in me and was suddenly called forth, or as an ability that was mine already but has come to be used with unusual power. It is the secret of the empowerment of the Holy Spirit that enhances the quality of the work of the church and distinguishes it from the quality of the world's activity. The Christian has an additional resource in the power of the Holy Spirit, which should make a crucial difference in his work.

The other dimension of gift is what might be called in group dynamics terms, group maintenance "gifts," for these are the gifts that emerge within the mission group which enable the group to maintain community, administer accountability, help persons to grow, and to get its task done.

The Holy Spirit is really *the* leader of a mission group and he calls out the gifts of leadership within the group. In this way the church does not assign leadership to a group, for all persons exercise in some way leadership in some area of the group's life.

If these group maintenance gifts are not called out, so that leadership in the many phases of the mission group's life is not called into existence, the group may end up with three people exercising their gifts and nine with unexercised gifts. And that breeds envy. So there are two types of gifts that need to be called out in persons; individual gifts for mission (a job that should begin in sharing groups), and group maintenance gifts which are called out within the mission group itself.

The beginning of a mission group is done by the "sounding of a call to mission" which may be done in a variety of ways. Many times the person just discovers another person within a sharing group with whom he can share his call in a variety of ways, such as personal conversation, and the two persons find that something common has sprung up within them. Another person may share his call at the Sunday morning worship service, or it may be shared with a particular organization in the life of the church. At any rate, the person simply indicates that he has sensed within himself a particular gift and that the nudgings of the Holy Spirit have led him to see or hear a particular area of mission, and he, in sounding the call, simply wants to know if anyone else has heard the same call to mission.

At this point a number of people may hear the call to mission, or a few, or none. If as many as three people hear the call to mission, then a process of affirming that mission group begins. If no one responds, then the person waits, nurturing his own insight into mission and prays for those who hear this particular need for ministry. For the time being he may have to pursue his call individually, exercising his gift for ministry and witness alone, until there emerge others, who out of gift, sense this same mission and join him.

This approach to developing a church program, as can be seen, in effect turns around the normal way of doing church programing. Normally, we, in church leadership positions, indicate a need, devise a program to meet the need, and then enlist and train persons to do the work, whether it is their gift or not. The mission group approach assumes that God has enough gifts within that church to get that particular church's part of the mission done, if only it will spend the time calling forth the gifts for ministry and witness. It then waits to see what the gifts are that will emerge. Then, it sets the program to match those gifts. This approach assumes that God is at work calling forth the gifts in that church that will be necessary for joining him in mission in that particular area of the world.

Mission groups are affirmed by the church council in The Church of the Saviour, but unlike most church councils its sole business is not administrative. Part of its business is the admission of new members into the life of the church and the confirming of the call to mission by groups that submit their sense of call to mission to this group for confirmation. Sometimes the church council discerns that this is just an "ego trip" by a person or group of persons, or that the time hasn't arrived for this mission to be seriously implemented. Thus, there is in this church council, made up of two representatives from each mission group, serving only a year at a time, a group of people who take seriously the "testing of the call to mission" so that there is a real seriousness to the commitment to mission on the part of those who have sounded the call, and those who test the call for its validity.

The same is true with regard to the mission groups in calling forth the gifts for group maintenance. The group decides on the validity of the call of persons to assume certain group functions. Sometimes the group will indicate that they have discerned a particular gift in a member of which he may or may not be aware. The group members, therefore, call forth the gift of a person becoming its spiritual growth director. At other times, a person will feel impressed to indicate this as their gift, and the mission group is called on to affirm or disaffirm that person's discernment of his/her own gift. Thus, the call to gift, both in terms of personal gift, the call to mission, and the maintenance gifts within the group, all are charisma from the Holy Spirit who gives power, and without which the group could not function as it confronts the power structures of the world.

Two additional elements about the call to mission and the gifts that emerge need to be mentioned. Persons must be prepared for the call to evolve, and they must be prepared for a call to a particular mission (my focus today) to not be my focus of mission five years from now. In the first instance, when the call to mission occurs, persons are not prepared to see all the implications of where that call to mission will lead them. In trying to respond to the call of mission to be a means of reconciliation between blacks and whites, the case study group did not foresee that they would be involved in opening up housing for blacks in normally middle-class, suburban, white neighborhoods. They simply had gone out to create better fellowship groups between black and white members of neighboring churches. But, the call to mission evolved as the Holy Spirit nudged them into new and more demanding areas of involvement. But, at each juncture there emerged the gifts to get that particular part of the call to mission accomplished.

So the form in which the call is usually heard is very simple, though seemingly impossible in terms of conventional wisdom. Then, the group starts being obedient to that call, and it begins to sense the implications of what is being dealt with, and new dimensions of the call to mission emerge and have to be dealt with, and the first thing you know a call to improve race relations among neighboring black and white churches has emerged into fair housing, quality education, equal job opportunity, and the political and economic structures which hold minority people in oppression. But, the Holy Spirit has been leading all the time and it is only gradually that you find yourself doing things you never thought you would be doing initially, because of the evolution of the call.

There is also the matter of a particular call shifting either for the individual or the group. Sometimes this shift means that mission groups come into being, and their need is fulfilled quickly, or has diminished in need, and the mission group disbands and a new call is issued and a new focus is begun. I do not mean by this that when a particular mission task becomes difficult, it is time to quit. What I am describing here is the fact that where God calls a person today may not be where he will call him five years from now. And, even his gifts for ministry and witness may shift as the call to mission changes. For some, who have planned for the certainty of a particular vocational commitment, or a particular area of ministry, for the rest of their lives, this may be a little too uncomfortable. But, the leadership of the Holy Spirit, as his nudgings continue to be pursued, plays an important part in the continual development of a flexibility of living and doing.

Group Structures and Structures of Obedience

How should mission groups be structured, both in terms of leadership structures and structures which hold the group in tension with itself and its mission of engagement—its structures of obedience? The necessary structures of leadership for a group should be only those necessary to: (1) get the task of mission done and (2) those necessary for the maintenance of the group's community, its belongingness to each other. Too much of the leadership structures in most church organizations today are there simply because someone in an office somewhere decided that was what was needed. By approaching leadership structures from the point of need, a group is free to explore what is needed in terms of structure for their particular group.

Therefore, in giving what has been effective in one situation should not be understood as that which is necessary for another group. The Church of the Saviour has found that each of their mission groups should have the following "gifts" which are exercised on behalf of the entire group: (1) a convenor-moderator (sometimes called a prior); (2) a spiritual growth director whose concern it is for maintaining the continuing Christian growth of its members; (3) a pastor-prophet whose dual role it is to both shepherd and to point the critical finger of admonition; (4) an activist, whose job it is to encourage the group in its mission work and to work at the administration of that task; and (5) a patron of gifts, whose gift it is to see, to call out, and affirm gifts in others, as Jesus did in Peter. Now, there are many other gifts within their mission groups, as each member exercises his gift of leadership. For example, one may exercise the gift of intercessory prayer or the gift of gathering information about the structures of society to which the mission group is ministering. There are as many gifts as are needed to get the job done, and each person has, within the group, his/her gift called out and affirmed by the group as it seeks to be channels of power of the Holy Spirit in ministering at that particular juncture of brokenness.

Since a mission group is committed to experiencing community, or engagement with one another in depth, not just a relationship built on the basis of friendship or human affinity, or even a vision of an "ideal community," then structures of obedience have to be built within the mission group to deal with the costly matter of accountability. Depth relationships in community are costly as God in his grace gives the gift of *koinonia*. Though community is built on the common experience of the reconciling grace in Jesus Christ, the building of a *depth community* in which God can give more abundantly of his fellowship gift of community means that the mission group has to grapple with what structures need to be created which will help the group members be responsible to the exercising of their gifts, to their mutual support of one another, and to the living out of the creative tension of being both an outward and an inward person.

Elizabeth O'Connor has said that the real failure of the church today, is not in the failure of interpretations, for there are many; but in the "pervading attitude in the Church itself that the inwardness of its life can be known without any serious commitment." [4] This is true in every aspect of a mission group's life. Most churches and mission groups who do not wrestle with the structures of obedience and commitment will eventually fail for no one wants to encounter their own, and others, resistance to those things that bind us and keep us from being free enough to be led in power by the Holy Spirit. There is a very serious need for a group to create within the group those means by which peers hold one another accountable and responsible without alienating them. Without these structures of obedience, the group is rendered powerless and its activity becomes the same quality of activity as the world's activity.

Group disciplines, which become part of the structures of obedience, should not become weights added upon members to weigh them down, but should be those embraced by the group members in such a fashion that the disciplines become "good news." They are those things that will help each individual achieve his own goal of inwardness and outwardness. Unless a person is at the point in his Christian pilgrimage that he is willing to live in a disciplined group life, he should not attempt to join a mission group but should wait until he hungers enough for that kind of life lived in depth that the disciplined way of life becomes "good news" for him.

Out of the sharing group, the mission group member had encountered what might be called "minimal disciplines" and the mission group will have expanded these, and modified them in making them more specific. But, the mission group now needs to go further unless it wants the group life to level off at just trying to keep the minimal disciplines. The mission group must also struggle with the concept of individual *maximum disciplines*, which are the application of continual Christian growth for each individual. This is the work of the spiritual growth director who, for each person, helps that person move beyond living at a minimal level to the exploration of his own Christian growth potential. O'Connor says, "nothing warrants the name discipline which does not evoke resistance, which means an opposing force comes into action." [5] Thomas Merton labeled this resistance, the encountering of "dread" as false images of self are encountered and stripped away, even those points of "infidelity to a personal demand of which one is dimly aware." [6]

O'Connor again says that disciplines need to be: balanced, specific, and definite; graduated to the needs of each person at their point of Christian pilgrimage. They should be applied at the point of internal readiness and not imposed, and be reviewed annually. Cosby says that the seeds of failure of many mission groups comes exactly at the point of not being willing to be specific at the point of disciplines. He points out that disciplines are not goals or aspirations to be worked toward, but serious commitments to be kept daily. So, in any mission group that takes its commitment seriously, and is powerful in its witness and ministry, there will be many different levels of disciplines going on at the same time as the spiritual growth director works with each person at his particular point of growth. But, none of them will drop below the common minimum discipline which governs the group's life.

Now, there is one more element to the structures of obedience that needs to be mentioned. How does a group hold each other accountable for the disciplines adopted and the commitment that each member has made? Some procedure of reporting has to be devised, either as a weekly written report shared with the spiritual growth director (and it may be possible for each person to have his own spiritual growth director, rather than the group having only one for the entire group), or a periodic verbal report shared with the group. A certain number of persons could be designated to share at each weekly meeting. But, some procedure has to be devised by the group by which accountability is built into the disciplined life that the mission group has embraced so that failures to keep a discipline may be noted, as well as the way in which God is dealing with a person through the Scriptures, and the crucial problems or mountaintop experiences which have been theirs for the past week.

Group Membership

I have already indicated that mission groups begin with the issuance of a call by a person or persons and is responded to by others. But, how shall group membership be determined at the beginning? How shall new members be added? Is it ever possible to leave the mission group? It would seem to me that initially group membership should be determined on the basis of hearing the call to that particular mission and some basic understanding of what the Christian faith is all about, both as to its past and as to its present demands in terms of discipleship. Members should also have some basic commitment to a life lived in a depth community and of being both an inward and outward person.

It would seem to me that a necessary pattern for having "sharing groups" and "mission groups" in the church as alternative structures, would include the following progression:

PREPARATORY STRUCTURES

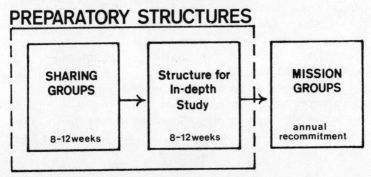

In this progression a person could initially join the process at *either* the point of sharing groups or the structure for in-depth study. But, it would be necessary for a person to have been in a sharing group for one eight-to-twelve week period, *plus* two basic courses in the study structure, *before* they go to a mission group. Though a person could join the preparatory structure at either point, two basic courses and one period in a sharing group is necessary before going into a mission group. This is necessary for a person to have experienced for at least a year, before joining a mission group, the following dimensions in his own life: indepth community; personal gifts for mission; the living out of a deep devotional life; exploration of self-awareness; basic Christian study; the discipline of obedience; what it means to live life out of a focused ministry; and God's call to his people to be on mission.

However, when a church is making its first attempt at a transition from sharing groups in the church to mission groups, the shift will not be as smooth as it can later be made when certain "preparatory structures," as mentioned above, are created. These preparatory structures would include sharing groups, plus in-depth courses of Christian study and spiritual formation, each of which would last for an eight-to-twelve week period and then begin again. In other words, both the sharing groups and the study groups would be eight to twelve weeks in duration. The in-depth study structure might include New Testament and Old Testament studies, ethics, church history, theology, devotional life, and personal self-examination and awareness.

But, the first time a church makes the transition from sharing groups to mission groups it may have to do much of the basic spiritual formation within the mission group itself or through a parallel organization created specifically for the spiritual formation of mission group members. Therefore, for a while, during the first transition, mission group members would be required to attend *both* the mission group and the spiritual formation group until some basic standard had been achieved. It might, then, be possible for the spiritual formation organization to continue as a preparatory structure for future mission groups *before* the mission groups actually began so that all new mission group members would have had a basic spiritual formation and some idea of their gifts for mission before beginning their involvement in mission groups.

It is not possible to use present church educational organizations for this task of spiritual formation. Though these organizations are meeting the needs of persons at different stages in their Christian pilgrimage, the level of commitment and personal discipline in the in-depth study structure is not the same. What would result is frustration among the mission group members who attempt to take seriously a discipline of study within existing church structures, where serious study is not the basic purpose of those organization's existence. It would also cause undue friction in those organizations to have someone impose upon the members of those educational organizations a depth of study that would be more burden than the "good news" which disciplines must be.

The admission of new members to mission groups which have been in existence for some time should be done at specific times during the year. Each mission group needs to have a core group of members who have heard the call to mission at that particular point where the mission group exists so that the integration of new members into the mission group can be orderly, both with regard to the continuance of the mission, and with regard to causing as little disruption to the depth of community achieved within the group.

It was indicated earlier that the adding of new members to sharing groups was not encouraged, yet with mission groups was possible. The difference is found in the fact that sharing groups are terminal, in that they have a time limit placed on them and each person within the group is still struggling with the degree of openness and honesty that can be risked.

In a mission group, because of its central core of committed members, there is already a deeper degree of those qualities because of the disciplines under which mission groups operate. However, there will be disruption when new members are brought into mission groups because anytime new persons are introduced into a group there is some renegotiation of relationships and a rerunning of each individual's past history in order to bring new persons up to date and to redo the interpersonal relationships between all the persons in the group. But, where a level of deep community life has already been achieved with some clear understandings of what is involved in being part of that mission group, as spelled out in the minimum disciplines, then there is a firmer ground on which to build a new community that includes new mission group members. This introduction of new members should not be done but once or twice a year, however, so that the disruption of the mission group is kept to a minimum.

Can you ever leave a mission group? Yes. Annually each mission group should provide an opportunity for persons in the mission group to recommit themselves to the mission group for another year. This provides a "trapdoor" for those who might otherwise feel trapped into an arena of mission which no longer holds meaning because of the evolvement of their own sense of mission and call, or because the disciplined group life has become no longer "good news" for them and they have to back off for a time of reexamination and reflection before seriously undertaking that kind of commitment in depth again. Recommitment also provides a time when the entire mission group takes stock of itself; the strength of their common call to mission; an evaluation of the group gifts; and the direction mission has taken during the past year.

One other word about group membership needs to be said. The temptation of mission groups, when they become engaged in mission and the enormity of the task becomes apparent, is to want to have as many persons involved in helping them accomplish the mission as possible. Cosby says that the first thing you know the mission group will start saying to persons who would like to be involved in the particular mission activity but are not committed to the disciplined community life necessary to the mission group, "come on and join us and you will find you will like it." This is just not the case. What happens is that persons who are invited in to "help" with the mission task before long begin to determine the agenda of the mission group, without understanding the reason that brought the mission group to its disciplined life in the first place. And, the group members have not helped the nonmembers face up to their own need for growth; they have just used them. So, as tempting as it is to invite everyone to join in mission, it is better to wait until persons come to the mission group with a clear understanding of what the committed group life is all about, and for the mission group to be content with that part of the mission that it has been given by God.

In group membership there should be as wide a variety of types of members as possible: young, old, married, the unmarried, rich, poor, educated, those with limited education. outgoing types, and inward types. In this way the heterogeneous mixture of persons will provide the widest possible variety of gifts for the performance of the group's mission.

Relationship to the Church

A mission group will meet weekly, other than those times when it is engaged in its work of mission, usually for one and a half to two hours in length. During that time, according to O'Connor the weekly meeting is divided into a worship time, a study time, and a sharing time. This is the meeting that gives the group its group "tone" for mission during the week. It may be that the mission of the group happens primarily on the weekend, or several nights during the week, so one night is set aside for the group's meeting where, not only study preparation for missions is done, but the group worships as a community (church really happens here) and it shares in the growth and nongrowth of its members.

Since mission group life is very costly, both in terms of personal commitment and time and involvement, it is easily seen that participation in the other organizational meetings of the normal church congregation is not possible outside of Sunday congregational worship and participation in the time of serious study in one of the structures for spiritual formation of the mission group members. For some church members involved in the other organizations of the church and some church leadership this means making an emotional adjustment and communicating what is happening in mission groups to the entire church body.

We have grown a generation of church members and leaders who have depended on statistical measurement, or numerical quantification, as the way to gauge a church's progress. With the kind of depth group and mission involvement described here, it is not possible for mission group members to attend every church function, nor to appear at the church every time the doors are opened. If an emotional adjustment can be made on the part of church leadership to this, and this can be properly interpreted to the larger church fellowship and new measurements of involvement determined, a church can succeed in the creation of and maintenance of alternative church structures in small sharing groups and mission groups. What is needed is a serious commitment on the part of church leadership and church membership alike to create and allow new structures to emerge within the life of the church which can begin to take seriously Christ's call to the mission of healing the brokenness of society.

Cosby summarized mission groups in 1958 when his church was struggling with this new form of church:

As I discover what aspect of that mission is mine, and as you discover your mission, and they happen to coincide, then we become part of a mission group. . . . Who cares what form it takes? Who knows what the details of it will be, when it meets and how it goes about its task? This is not important. The important thing is that this group discover the guidance of God step by step, and be so attuned to His will, and so flexible that it shall be able to discover what He has in mind. This is all you mean by a mission group: Two or more persons who have been grasped by the same concept of God's task for them, and who have been grasped by God, which is deeper and more profound than being grasped by a concept."

Taking hold of this idea of mission groups emerging where sharing groups have existed in the lives of thousands of people in churches over the last few years, could begin a new dimension as exciting (and maybe as controversial) as when Sunday Schools were first proposed nearly two hundred years ago.

Postscript

Some final words now need to be added about mission groups, especially in light of their evolvement from sharing groups. These need to be said as a "postscript" for it is only in working through the concepts of mission groups that these words about evolvement take on any meaning.

Sharing groups, or in-depth study structures, are of necessity preparatory structures for mission groups. They enable a person to "taste" new dimensions of the Christian faith. Persons come to preparatory structures out of a sense of hunger in the first place, and preparatory structures serve to point the direction towards real food for that hunger.

But, there comes a time in either type of preparatory structure that the food that is served there no longer completely satisfies. The elements of deeper growth and commitment to mission are missing. Consequently, persons become aware of a need to "move on." Usually, at some point in the preparatory structure, and certainly in mission groups, another level of disillusionment takes place. This phase of disillusionment has to do with a necessary "letting go" process that can only be described as "holy abandonment." This happens with regard to a person's own life as he tries to hold on to what are increasingly apparently fake images of discipleship and Christian community.

Bonhoeffer described this process in *Life Together* concerning what it takes to reach real Christian community:

Innumerable times a whole Christian community has broken down because it has sprung from a wish dream. The serious Christian, set down for the first time in a Christian community, is likely to bring with him a very definite idea of what Christian life together should be and to try to realize it. But God's grace speedily shatters such dreams. Just as surely as God desires to lead us to a knowledge of genuine Christian fellowship, so surely must we be overwhelmed by a great disillusionment with others, with Christians in general, and if we are fortunate, with ourselves.

By sheer grace, God will not permit us to live even for a brief period in a dream world. He does not abandon us to those rapturous experiences and lofty moods that come over us like a dream. God is not a God of the emotions [alone] but the God of truth [also]. Only that fellowship which faces such disillusionment, with all its unhappy and ugly aspects, begins to be what it should be in God's sight, begins to grasp in faith the promise that is given to it. The sooner this shock of disillusionment comes to an individual and to a community, the better for both. A community which cannot bear and cannot survive such a crisis, which insists upon keeping its illusion when it should be shattered, permanently loses in that moment the promise of Christian community. Sooner or later it will collapse. Every human wish dream that is injected into the Christian community is a hindrance to genuine community and must be banished if genuine community is to survive. He who loves his dream of a community more than the Christian community itself becomes a destroyer of the latter, even though his personal intentions may be ever so honest and earnest and sacrificial." [7]

The "letting go" process also is related to personal Christian growth and the devotional life. Other persons have described this painful, but necessary, letting go process in such books as *Contemplative Prayer,* where Thomas Merton talks of the ministry of spiritual "dread"; *Dark Night of the Soul,* by John of the Cross in which he speaks of the purging of human sensing in order to allow spiritual dimensions to take over; and *Interior Castle* by Teresa of Avila in which she describes a journey deeper and deeper into a deeper spiritual relationship with our Lord. Elizabeth O'Connor has also described this "letting go" in modern terms in three books: *A Search for Silence; Our Many Selves;* and *The Eighth Day of Creation.*

Thus, the journey into a deeper and richer Christian pilgrimage begins in hunger; continues to the point where we recreate an "ideal" church, of Christian life; a disillusionment with the achievement or agreement on the ideal; and a final "letting go" in order that God may create in us and through us something that is designed by his will.

Notes

1. Gordon Cosby, The Vineyard Renewal Conference, Louisville, Kentucky, September, 1972. Much of the material in this chapter grows out of the five conferences Cosby has given at The Vineyard since 1964, for which I am gratefully indebted.

2. Quoted in Kelly, *A Testament of Devotion,* p. 52.

3. Kelly, *op. cit.,* pp. 52-53.

4. O'Connor, *Our Many Selves,* p. 9.

5. O'Connor, *Journey Inward, Journey Outward,* p. 21.

6. Merton, *Contemplative Prayer,* p. 97.

7. Bonhoeffer, *Life Together,* pp. 16-17.

11 Small Groups—Alternative Structures in the Church

An alternative is defined as the stating of another possibility without invoking the discontinuity of past or present solutions. As opposed to revolution, the stating of alternatives says that the old does not have to be overthrown for new possibilities to emerge and seriously be considered alongside traditional forms.

The church needs to be committed to the exploration of alternatives through which God can build those new wineskins capable of holding the new wine that is being poured out on his people today. For those who are dissatisfied with a meaningless devotional life; for those exploring ways to communicate with an alienated culture; for those seeking a relevant church education program; for those searching out a different leadership and life-style from the win/lose syndrome of today's competitive society; for couples wanting to move beyond the shallowness of an institutionalized marriage relationship into the fullness of a caring relationship; for "dusty Christians" along the pilgrimage who seek deeper levels of spiritual existence; and for prophets who cry out "Is there anyone else out there"; for these and many others who are being called by their despair and disillusionment into new and deeper levels of ministry and witness, the small group can become the means for the exploration of alternatives for personal Christian living and for the community of faith, the church.

Renewal is speaking to the possibility of God's alternatives for persons and churches today.

The call to alternatives is a call to new and deeper relationships with God and fellowmen. Many times this call to alternatives may lead to failure, and those who are free enough to fail recognize failure as one way in which God instructs his people. But, the call to alternatives is after all a call to live by faith; to swing out on the trapeze bar with only the assurance that God has already swung the other bar to meet you. Then you have to let go, believing that the timing of "letting go" of one and "taking hold" of the other, are timed precisely.

On the other hand the call to alternatives recognizes that success may not always be measured by the criteria of "bigger and better." Success may simply mean that a life has been turned around and opened up, or that a church has found an authentic expression of discipleship.

The way of alternatives also means that what emerges in one place is not *the* form to be used by every other person or church in renewal. The way of alternatives is the way of openness to the Holy Spirit's guidance, openness to the agenda of the world around, and a freedom to be led. In this way God's alternatives emerge in such a variety that copying the sameness of another's solution, or living the rigid life of principles, becomes not an openness to freedom and to the searching out of God's alternatives that are rich with *karios* moments, but a life lived out of fear of a faithwalk with God.

Yesterday's approaches to religion are not adequate for tomorrow's demands on the faith. Thus, the way into the future is by faith, open to what the future holds, not the clinging on to the past as if the church "was an ancient museum and we only the curators of it." The richness of God's future for his people is found in a willingness to be open to his leadership now; a willingness to search out the different solutions of discipleship; a willingness to ask the embarrassing questions; a willingness to explore what has not been and say "why not?"

There continue to emerge among God's people everywhere persons who are exploring the unknown dimensions of the Christian faith, and who are coming up with alternatives that are as exciting and demanding on this generation as yesterday's solutions were for the past generation. And, these alternatives are being explored primarily through small searching and support groups.[1]

Small Groups As Alternative Structures Within the Church

Small groups, whether they be sharing groups, in-depth study structures, or mission groups, become within the life of the church alternative structures, and I believe that it is best to deal with them in this approach. This simply means that they exist side-by-side with the existing educational structures and offer to the church member options for personal Christian growth and involvement.

By dealing with small groups as alternative structures within the total life of the church, two problems have been dealt with. First, the church, in facilitating and encouraging small groups, is doing so within the normal life of the church and not forcing them to have to exist independently of, or outside of, the main-stream of the life of the church. Secondly, the church has faced up to one of the more serious concerns of renewal by dealing with the whole system of renewal. Renewal is systemic. By that I mean, the church is a whole system of things that relate and interrelate with each other. Those who have thought they could deal with only one area of renewal, such as a particular social issue, or just the use of small sharing groups in the church, have come to much grief when they found out that what was happening as they dealt with one renewal concern, such as a social issue, or the emergence of small groups, really was producing at the same time "waves" in other areas of the church's life.

We have seen too many people who have had genuine, authentic experiences at renewal conferences, where they have been changed and new life has emerged, but, when they went back into structures which were not responsive to this new that was emerging in them, encountered real difficulties. As a consequence, some just became apathetic and gave up on change ever happening in the church with any depth, and others simply just gave up on the church and left it. Pastors, and other church leaders have sensed this, and many have dealt with the problem from one of two stances. Either they identified so heavily and readily with those who were coming alive in the small group structures that their entire ministry was turned in that direction, to the neglect of the rest of the congregation (which were very often the largest part and the more financially endowed). This then produced such hostility among the rest of the congregation that the pastor was forced to leave, sometimes with the small group who had just begun to find a new sense of authentic, vital Christianity. Often these groups that pulled out became "house churches." Or, because of increased despair and disillusionment which later set in, the whole experiment failed, becoming a further illustration of the hopelessness of renewing that ancient relic of civilization called the church.

The other course of action taken by church leadership has been to avoid the whole renewal and small group "thing" as if it were a briar patch and they the fox chasing an illusive rabbit. When the mention of small groups came up, all they could think of was that the groups might be divisive—they thought they had heard someone say at the last pastors' conference how small groups were tearing up his church.

It seems to me that a solution that continues to gain acceptability and workability is the one built on the concept of renewal having to deal with the entire system of a church. This is a very difficult task and one that frightens many from attempting renewal, for it means dealing with subjects that were never taught in the seminary. It means dealing with the "systems" of a church, knowing where power is located, and how to effect change, a theory of change. And, yet, the pastor, trying to be the pastor of the entire church, not just of those who keep the traditional structures, nor just pastor of those who are innovating and trying out new modes of expressing Christian discipleship, finds trying to balance the entire church system a difficult, yet necessary, task.

Small groups should be considered by the church leadership as "alternative structures," which emerge and exist alongside of existing structures. They should be given room, along with those existing structures, to live and begin to meet the needs of persons who are finding new life through small groups without in any way indicating that one structure is superior and more authentic than the other. People are at different stages in their personal Christian pilgrimage. This approach of allowing the new and the existing to stand side by side recognizes that those who wish to explore new dimensions of the Christian faith, to the extent to which God gives them the grace to understand and appropriate it are encouraged in that direction.

The approach of "alternative structures" also says that some persons in the church may never feel compelled to move into those new waters. And, so a church provides for them through those existing structures which meet their needs at that particular point in their Christian experience. If a pastor and other church leadership is fulfilling the commandment of Jesus to Peter, which has become the commandment of everyone who assumes the equipping or enabling role of vocational church ministers, "Feed my sheep," they will always try to provide that creative tension necessary to move Christians into deeper and deeper experiences of the faith. Most of us as church leaders have been content to expect only what could be described as what the "average Christian" can do without ever asking the question, "What are the highest dimensions of 'Christian potential?'" It would seem to me that settling only for the average may never produce the long distance runners of the faith of which the church is in such desperate need today.

Thus small groups, as an "alternative structure," can help overcome the problem of having people who have been changed by a deep renewal dimension in their lives, but have not found the structure within which to express that new discovery. Genuine renewal results in a new life-style; old values and modes of living will no longer satisfy. Thus, as we seek to open people up to new and deeper dimensions of faith and discipleship, we need to provide those on-going structures within which we can also allow the new to be expressed. Small groups, where both the elements of personal and structural renewal come together, seem to offer that possibility.

It is simply not enough to expect the renewal of God's people to happen by having lay weekends or renewal retreats once or twice a year. The structures through which the new discoveries can be expressed has to be grappled with, or all the efforts of personal renewal is like trying to pour new wine back into old wineskins—the old containers will be broken and the new wine of newly discovered dimensions of Christian faith are lost, sometimes forever (Luke 5:37-39). Jesus continually spoke of the need to deal with both dimensions of the new life; its personal dimensions and the structural means through which it would be expressed. At one point in his ministry he had to drive this need home very forcefully when he told the sellers of religious goods to "clear out" of the Court of the Gentiles where selling and merchandising was going on. In doing so he was announcing the restoration of the mission to the Gentiles, as God had originally intended; and that Israel, in missing its calling to mission, had turned that place for Gentile worship into a place of commerce (John 2:13-17).

He challenged leadership patterns by telling his disciples that they were not to "lord it over" others as was the accepted pattern of religious and political leadership of the day. He challenged the patterns of sabbath observance and of giving; and even the place of worship "neither on this mountain nor in Jerusalem" (John 4:21), but wherever people gathered in two's and three's and sought the Father in spirit and in truth. The final dramatization of Jesus' work of structural renewal, as well as personal spiritual renewal, came when the Temple veil was split into two pieces, and a structure that had been established at the very beginning of the nation Israel itself came to an end. God was approachable now. No longer would it require the ministry of a special man, and then only once a year. Through Jesus Christ we had one with whom we could share communion with the Father. Small groups become for churches alternative structures which can deal effectively with the two dimensions of personal and structural renewal.

Administering Alternative Structures

Church leadership, especially the pastor and minister of education, have the primary responsibility for the failure or success of small groups emerging within the life of a church. I have seen churches where a lay renewal weekend began a new dimension of life in that church, but a few months later when you asked persons in the church what had happened since, a shrug of the shoulders told the sad story of a lack of church leadership support. Renewal, whether personal or structural, begins with the work of the Holy Spirit. But, church leadership can smother those fires of new life or be the encouragers and enablers of new life emerging.

The first task of administering alternative structures is to recognize hunger among the members, to encourage that hunger (even when it is unrecognized by the person, himself) through the planning of events in the life of the church which will call forth the hunger, and to create the structures that feed the hunger. In other words, church leadership has the responsibility for being the encourager and enabler of hunger as a way of leading people to deeper levels of personal Christian growth.

Secondly, church leadership must grapple with the two dimensions of personal and structural renewal at the same time. Otherwise, what has been begun in personal spiritual renewal will be lost. Therefore, as persons are opened up to personal spiritual renewal through lay weekends, renewal retreats, and conferences, "back at the church" the church leadership must be prepared to be the encouragers and enablers (not the "enlisters" who are promoting everybody join a small group!) of those who wish to continue in a sharing group. Then, as those who are staying in close touch with the sharing groups, church leadership should be prepared for that moment of transition when persons need to move into the in-depth study structure, or into mission groups (grouped around a specific call to mission). This means not only helping people move to those alternative structures that will meet their needs at a particular point in their own journey, but anticipating the meeting of those needs through helping people create the appropriate structures to meet the need.

Thirdly, the question of how does church leadership stay in touch must be fully explored. My personal belief is that sharing groups, in-depth study structures, and mission groups ought to be "trusted" so that a day-by-day monitoring is not done, But, the development of a sensitivity to the progress, or lack of progress, of a group becomes the arena of ministry of church leadership so that assistance can be given when needed. Also, alternative structures should be administered through a "group representatives' council" (two persons from each group), which would meet weekly with the pastor, or minister of education, on the work of the groups. This should be a time of sharing between the group representatives (and this position should be rotated each six months—maybe half the council being rotated each six months—for mission groups and in-depth study structures, but each six weeks for sharing groups, in order for there to be freshness to the council) as to what God is doing in their groups.

In addition, once or twice a quarter there might be a meeting of all the groups to give a greater sense of identity and commonness to those involved in these alternative structures. This could be a time of input by the church leadership to the entire group, or by one of the group leaders. Also a large amount of time should be spent on sharing from each group so that other groups can get a feel of what is going on in the other alternative structures.

Fourthly, church leadership needs to work closely with those in mission groups and those staffing the in-depth study structure, to see that the dimensions of in-depth personal growth are being maintained. This might be a meeting of the mission group that maintains the in-depth study structure (a group of people who have the gift of teaching and feel called to this ministry), or a meeting of the spiritual growth directors of each mission group.

Finally, in administering alternative structures, church leadership need to facilitate the flow of productive communications between alternative structures and existing church organizations. This needs to be done at several levels. There is the level of communicating the need for alternative structures in the first place; the need to keep the entire congregation aware of what is going on in alternative structures; and the interpretation of the apparent noninvolvement of persons in alternative structures in the other activities of the church, with the exception of corporate worship on Sunday morning and the in-depth study structure.

Administering alternative structures, then, calls for a sensitivity on the part of church leadership to the work of God's Holy Spirit as he moves among his people calling them to new and deeper dimensions of the faith. And, it invites persons to create, encourage, and nurture the growth of other structures as a means for meeting a deeper hunger among God's people.

Alternative Structures—A Door into the Future

Martin Marty, in a recent conference at The Vineyard, said: "We are too far into a major cultural revolution in our society, which is already shaking the very foundations of many of our long established institutions, including the church, to continue to believe exclusively that the old forms will survive as they presently exist today. Yet, at the same time, we are not far enough into that cultural shift to have invented the new forms that will really work." [2]

What do you do in the meantime? I believe that you hold onto the old while at the same time creating the new, alternative structures, which can become a door into the future. Someone may ask, "How long before we know what *the* new will look like?" My answer is maybe never. Maybe, if we are free enough to be led of God's Holy Spirit into new and deeper levels of Christian experience, we will also be free enough to allow for a variety of shapes to emerge so that God's new people will take seriously the "call to variety" which is implied in the giving of the charisma (gifts) to each person and each congregation in a different way for the meeting of the needs of mission in that particular locale.

However, the decade of the 1960's, which was rich in renewal understandings, has provided some clues for the new that is already emerging all around us, and which may be part of the new personal and church life-style of future Christianity—a door into the future. Basically, these twelve renewal understandings have been attempts to get at the need for the church to be both fellowship and mission. They are places where, in small groups, persons have been exploring new dimensions of what it means to live at increasingly deeper levels of Christ's call to discipleship.

1. The need for *structural renewal* was one of the earliest cries of the renewal movement as tired, out-of-date structures were no longer able to respond to the new demands being made on the church. New directions were proposed and this area of renewal continues to occupy much of the concern of many renewalists today. It is interesting that almost every major religious body in America is presently undergoing "reorganization." With all of this interest in structural renewal much remains to be done in helping the local church restructure its life.

2. The *recovery of mission* in the life of the church was the heart of many 1960 studies, and an entire group of books examined this concern in the life of the church. Mission-action became a byword for many groups in the church.

3. The basic understanding that the *ministry belongs to the*

laity, and the concomitant recovery of the equipping ministry as central in the function of the clergy, was discussed over and over again in the 1960's. Elton Trueblood in 1952 had said that if the ministry of the ordinary Christian could be recovered in the same manner that the Bible was opened up to the ordinary people four hundred years ago, a new Reformation would take place. Likewise, the study of the Bible passage, Ephesians 4:11-12, began a whole new understanding of the role of pastor as the enabler of the church members for their ministry.

4. A need for *integrity and authenticity concerning social issues* at a time when there seemed to be so much disparity between the gospel's demands and what was going on in the lives of persons, churches, and denominations focused even more sharply the fact that ministry was central to the life of the church. The need to attempt a ministry of reconciliation to the oppressed arose because of the issues which challenged society and the church, such as the racial confrontations and the Vietnam war. Books like *The Cost of Discipleship, The Secular City,* and *The Suburban Captivity of the Church* aroused the hunger of many for a renewed church that was socially responsive.

5. Relational theology focused on the need to build *deep and meaningful relationships* among persons. This was the concern of many, especially Bruce Larson, Ralph Osborne, Lyman Coleman, Keith Miller and others. These began to develop new understandings about the church as a fellowship; a real community of believers. They taught us that to be fully human begins with liking ourselves as the handiwork of God. The use of the small group, the retreat weekend, relational Bible study, relational teaching, and the place of self-reflection have all come as tools of relational theology.

6. Another emphasis has been on the *renewal of the evangelistic witness* through the Lay Witness Mission. Developed by Ben Campbell Johnson, it uses a lay renewal team who go into a local church on a weekend, and through small group sharing sessions and meetings at the church, share their witness of what they are experiencing of God's work in their lives. The impact of this form of evangelistic renewal has already been felt by thousands of churches of all denominations as lay people form

teams, paying their own way to share with other lay people what God is doing in their lives. Thus, renewal has been defined for thousands of lay people as a new experience of a living testimony of Christ's presence in their lives.

7. Another definition came primarily through the efforts of the Church of the Saviour in Washington, D.C., where Gordon Cosby and Elizabeth O'Connor have led many of us to see that the renewal starting point is at the *deepening of the devotional life.* Influenced heavily by Quaker Douglas Steere (and therefore by a whole line of Quaker pietists: John Woolman, Rufus Jones, and Thomas Kelly, as well as by other Christian mystics), they have given us the combined elements of the search for self through introspection with a new appreciation for Bible study, prayer, and time spent in silence with God. These are combined in what they have called the "critical minimum" for balancing the "journey outward" (a life lived in mission in society) with the "journey inward" (a life lived out of the deep center of relationship with God).

8. Also from the Church of the Saviour have come insights into the *integrity of church membership* where membership in a local church is simply not taken for granted, and requirements for church membership are worked out in a disciplined fellowship. This also was the viewpoint of the book by Findley Edge, *A Quest for Vitality in Religion.*

9. The *charismatic renewal* has probably received more notoriety than other phases of renewal with its emphasis upon the indwelling presence and power of the Holy Spirit. Unfortunately such concerns as speaking in tongues has in many ways overshadowed the other concerns of charismatic renewalists in their emphasis on being Spirit-indwelt, Spirit-directed, and the calling out of spiritual gifts for ministry and witness.

10. The renewal of worship, or *liturgical renewal,* began early in the decade of the 1960's. The recovery of celebration in the worship experiences of the church has replaced the often drab and dead formalities of Sunday worship. The use of folk musicals, instruments other than a piano and organ, conversation prayer, banners, light shows, the removal of pews, the building of more sanctuaries in the round, the use of lay people as worship leaders,

and the formation of worship committees to work with the pastor in building the worship experience on behalf of all the people—these and other innovations have given new dimensions to God's worshipping people.

11. The *renewal of the teaching ministry of the church* begins with the basic understanding that God's people are to be equipped for ministry and witness (Eph. 4:12). It takes seriously two other renewal understandings: (1) that mission is central to the life of the church; and (2) that ministry belongs to the laity. It does not believe that Christian education is an end in itself or is to be used by the church to engrandize itself (thus making the church a consumer of the church's ministry and witness). Therefore, education is for equipping God's people for mission in the world.

12. The issue of *creative simplicity* in personal and corporate Christian living is being raised with increased vigor today. Persons are becoming more and more aware of the fact that the world does not have an unlimited supply of resources, nor is there an equal distribution of the world's resources so that everyone's basic needs are adequately met. Thus creative simplicity becomes both an examination of what is enough, as well as how do I share with those who do not have basic needs when I have an over-abundance of resources. This is a crucial question for this nation which consumes out of proportion to the world's population the available natural resources of the world. This is a renewal question that deeply affects the life-style in which Christians and churches live.

Conclusion

Renewal is a call to exploring alternatives; to growth; to being free to be led to an emerging personal and corporate Christian life-style. As Thomas Merton has put it: "The mind that is the prisoner of conventional ideas, and the will that is the captive of its own desire cannot accept the seeds of an unfamiliar truth and a supernatural desire. For how can I receive the seeds of freedom if I am in love with slavery and how can I cherish the desire of God if I am filled with another and an opposite desire? God cannot plant His liberty in me because I am prisoner and I do not even desire to be free. I love my captivity and I imprison myself in the desire for the things that I hate, and I have hardened my heart against true love. I must learn therefore to let go of the familiar and the usual and consent to what is new and unknown to me. I must learn to 'leave myself' in order to find myself by yielding to the love of God. If I were looking for God, every event and every moment would sow, in my will, grains of His life that would spring up one day in a tremendous harvest." [3]

Hungry people meeting in sharing groups, studying in depth the Christian faith, and meeting the brokenness of society through mission groups, is a call to a personal and corporate "letting go" in order that God, through the empowerment of his Holy Spirit, can recreate a new people for the needs of our broken society today. It is a call to new and deeper dimensions of being free to be led; a new Christian life-style.

NOTES

1. Some of the material in this chapter was originally presented in "The Winepress," Newsletter of The Vineyard Conference Center, Louisville, Kentucky.

2. Martin Marty, The Vineyard Renewal Conference, Louisville, Kentucky, October, 1972.

3. Merton, *New Seeds of Contemplation* (New York: A New Directions Book, 1961), p. 16.

SUGGESTIONS FOR FURTHER READING

COMMUNITY

Bonhoeffer, Dietrich. *The Communion of Saints*. New York: Harper & Row, 1963.
_____. *The Cost of Discipleship*. New York: The Macmillan Company, 1959.
_____. *Life Together*. London: SCM Press, LTD, 1954.
Howe, Reuel L. *The Miracle of Dialogue*. New York: The Seabury Press, 1963.
Mayerhoff, Milton. *On Caring*. New York: Harper & Row, 1971.
O'Connor, Elizabeth. *Call to Commitment*. New York: Harper & Row, 1963.
_____. *Journey Inward, Journey Outward*. New York: Harper & Row, 1968.
Steere, Douglas V. *On Being Present Where You Are*. Wallingford, Penn.: Pendle Hill Publications, 1967.

CHURCH RENEWAL

Edge, Findley B. *The Greening of the Church*. Waco: Word Books, 1971.
_____. *A Quest for Vitality in Religion*. Nashville: Broadman Press, 1963.
Girard, Robert C. *Brethren, Hang Loose*. Grand Rapids: Zondervan, 1972.
Haney, David. *Breakthrough into Renewal*. Nashville: Broadman Press, 1974.
_____. *The Idea of the Laity*. Grand Rapids: Zondervan, 1973.
_____. *Renew My Church*. Grand Rapids: Zondervan, 1972.
Larson, Bruce and Osborne, Ralph. *The Emerging Church*. Waco: Word Books, 1970.
Marty, Martin E. *The Fire We Can Light*. New York: Doubleday, 1973.
Richards, Lawrence O. *A New Face for the Church*. Grand Rapids: Zondervan, 1970.

DEVOTIONAL LIFE

Haughey, John C. *The Conspiracy of God: The Holy Spirit in Men*. New York: Doubleday, 1973.
Hinson, E. Glenn. *Seekers After Mature Faith*. Waco: Word Books, 1968.
_____. *A Serious Call to a Contemplative Lifestyle*. Philadelphia: Westminster Press, (to be released Fall, 1974).
Kelly, Thomas R. *A Testament of Devotion*. New York: Harper & Row, 1941.
Kierkegaard, Soren. *Purity of Heart*. New York: Harper Torchbacks, 1948.
Merton, Thomas. *Contemplative Prayer*. New York: Doubleday Image Books, 1971.
_____. *New Seeds of Contemplation*. New York: New Directions, 1961.
O'Connor, Elizabeth. *Search for Silence*. Waco: Word Books, 1972.
Quoist, Michel. *Prayers*. New York: Sheed & Ward, 1963.
Steere, Douglas. *On Beginning from Within* and *Listening to Another*. New York: Harper & Row, 1964.
_____. *Dimensions of Prayer*. Nashville: Woman's Division of Christian Service, Board of Missions, United Methodist Church, 1962.

158

PERSONAL RENEWAL

Larson, Bruce. *Ask Me to Dance*. Waco: Word Books, 1972.
———. *Living on the Growing Edge*. Grand Rapids: Zondervan, 1968.
———. *No Longer Strangers*. Waco: Word Books, 1971.
———. *Setting Men Free*. Grand Rapids: Zondervan, 1967.
Miller, Keith. *The Becomers*. Waco: Word Books, 1973.
———. *A Second Touch*. Waco: Word Books, 1967.
———. *Taste of New Wine*. Waco: Word Books, 1965.
Olsson, Karl. *Come to the Party*. Waco: Word Books, 1972.

SELF-AWARENESS

Berne, Eric. *Games People Play*. New York: Grove Press, 1964.
Harris, Thomas A. *I'm OK, You're OK*. New York: Harper & Row, 1969.
James, Muriel. *Born to Love*. Reading, Mass.: Addison-Wesley, 1973.
——— and Jongeward, Dorothy. *Born to Win*. Reading, Mass.: Addison-Wesley Pub. Co., 1971.
Jourard, Sidney M. *The Transparent Self*. New York: Van Nostrand Reinhold Co., 1971.
Madden, Myron C. *The Power to Bless*. Nashville: Abingdon Press, 1970.
Nouwen, Henri J. *The Wounded Healer*. New York: Doubleday, 1972.
———. *With Open Hands*. Notre Dame, Ind.: Ave Maria Press, 1972.
O'Connor, Elizabeth. *Our Many Selves*. New York: Harper & Row, 1971.
Powell, John. *Why Am I Afraid to Tell You Who I Am?* Chicago: Argus, 1969.
———. *Why Am I Afraid to Love?* Chicago: Argus, 1972.
Tournier, Paul. *A Place for You*. London: SCM Press, 1968.

GIFTS

O'Connor, Elizabeth. *Eighth Day of Creation*. Waco: Word Books, 1971.

SMALL GROUPS

Casteel, John L., ed. *The Creative Role of Interpersonal Groups in the Church Today*. New York: Association Press, 1968.
Clinebell, Howard J., Jr. *The People Dynamic*. New York: Harper & Row, 1972.
Coleman, Lyman. *Acts Alive*. Waco: Creative Resources, 1971.
———. *Breaking Free*. Waco: Creative Resources, 1971.
———. *Celebration*. Waco: Creative Resources, 1972.
———. *The Coffee House Itch*. Waco: Creative Resources, 1972.
———. *Discovery*. Waco: Creative Resources, 1971.
———. *Groups in Action*. Waco: Creative Resources, 1971.
———. *Kaleidoscope*. Waco: Creative Resources, 1972.
———. *Man Alive*. Waco: Creative Resources, 1972.
———. *Rap*. Waco: Creative Resources, 1972.
———. *Serendipity*. Waco: Creative Resources, 1972.
Dow, Robert Arthur. *Learning Through Encounter*. Valley Forge: Judson Press, 1971.
Goble, Frank. *The Third Force*. New York: Pocket Book, 1971.
Leslie, Robert C. *Sharing Groups in the Church*. Nashville: Abingdon Press, 1971.
Oden, Thomas C. *The Intensive Group Experience, The New Pietism*. Philadelphia: The Westminster Press, 1972.
Reid, Clyde. *Groups Alive—Church Alive*. New York: Harper & Row, 1969.

Richards, Lawrence O. *69 Ways to Start a Study Group and Keep It Growing.* Grand Rapids: Zondervan, 1973.
Rogers, Carl. *On Encounter Groups.* New York: Harper & Row, 1970.

MISSION

Ellul, Jacques. *The Presence of the Kingdom.* New York: Seabury Press, 1967.
————. *False Presence of the Kingdom.* New York: Seabury Press, 1972.
————. *The Politics of God and the Politics of Man.* Grand Rapids: Eerdmans, 1972.
Stringfellow, William. *Count It All Joy.* Grand Rapids: Eerdmans, 1967.
————. *Dissenter in a Great Society.* Nashville: Abingdon Press, 1966.
————. *Free in Obedience.* New York: Seabury Press, 1964.
————. *A Private and Public Faith.* Grand Rapids: Eerdmans, 1962.
————. *An Ethic for Christians and Other Aliens in a Strange Land.* Waco: Word Books, 1973.
Yoder, John Howard. *Politics of Jesus.* Grand Rapids: Eerdmans, 1972.

PERSONAL RENEWAL

Larson, Bruce. *Ask Me to Dance*. Waco: Word Books, 1972.
_____. *Living on the Growing Edge*. Grand Rapids: Zondervan, 1968.
_____. *No Longer Strangers*. Waco: Word Books, 1971.
_____. *Setting Men Free*. Grand Rapids: Zondervan, 1967.
Miller, Keith. *The Becomers*. Waco: Word Books, 1973.
_____. *A Second Touch*. Waco: Word Books, 1967.
_____. *Taste of New Wine*. Waco: Word Books, 1965.
Olsson, Karl. *Come to the Party*. Waco: Word Books, 1972.

SELF-AWARENESS

Berne, Eric. *Games People Play*. New York: Grove Press, 1964.
Harris, Thomas A. *I'm OK, You're OK*. New York: Harper & Row, 1969.
James, Muriel. *Born to Love*. Reading, Mass.: Addison-Wesley, 1973.
_____ and Jongeward, Dorothy. *Born to Win*. Reading, Mass.: Addison-Wesley Pub. Co., 1971.
Jourard, Sidney M. *The Transparent Self*. New York: Van Nostrand Reinhold Co., 1971.
Madden, Myron C. *The Power to Bless*. Nashville: Abingdon Press, 1970.
Nouwen, Henri J. *The Wounded Healer*. New York: Doubleday, 1972.
_____. *With Open Hands*. Notre Dame, Ind.: Ave Maria Press, 1972.
O'Connor, Elizabeth. *Our Many Selves*. New York: Harper & Row, 1971.
Powell, John. *Why Am I Afraid to Tell You Who I Am?* Chicago: Argus, 1969.
_____. *Why Am I Afraid to Love?* Chicago: Argus, 1972.
Tournier, Paul. *A Place for You*. London: SCM Press, 1968.

GIFTS

O'Connor, Elizabeth. *Eighth Day of Creation*. Waco: Word Books, 1971.

SMALL GROUPS

Casteel, John L., ed. *The Creative Role of Interpersonal Groups in the Church Today*. New York: Association Press, 1968.
Clinebell, Howard J., Jr. *The People Dynamic*. New York: Harper & Row, 1972.
Coleman, Lyman. *Acts Alive*. Waco: Creative Resources, 1971.
_____. *Breaking Free*. Waco: Creative Resources, 1971.
_____. *Celebration*. Waco: Creative Resources, 1972.
_____. *The Coffee House Itch*. Waco: Creative Resources, 1972.
_____. *Discovery*. Waco: Creative Resources, 1971.
_____. *Groups in Action*. Waco: Creative Resources, 1971.
_____. *Kaleidoscope*. Waco: Creative Resources, 1972.
_____. *Man Alive*. Waco: Creative Resources, 1972.
_____. *Rap*. Waco: Creative Resources, 1972.
_____. *Serendipity*. Waco: Creative Resources, 1972.
Dow, Robert Arthur. *Learning Through Encounter*. Valley Forge: Judson Press, 1971.
Goble, Frank. *The Third Force*. New York: Pocket Book, 1971.
Leslie, Robert C. *Sharing Groups in the Church*. Nashville: Abingdon Press, 1971.
Oden, Thomas C. *The Intensive Group Experience*, The New Pietism. Philadelphia: The Westminster Press, 1972.
Reid, Clyde. *Groups Alive—Church Alive*. New York: Harper & Row, 1969.

Richards, Lawrence O. *69 Ways to Start a Study Group and Keep It Growing.* Grand Rapids: Zondervan, 1973.
Rogers, Carl. *On Encounter Groups.* New York: Harper & Row, 1970.

MISSION
Ellul, Jacques. *The Presence of the Kingdom.* New York: Seabury Press, 1967.
————. *False Presence of the Kingdom.* New York: Seabury Press, 1972.
————. *The Politics of God and the Politics of Man.* Grand Rapids: Eerdmans, 1972.
Stringfellow, William. *Count It All Joy.* Grand Rapids: Eerdmans, 1967.
————. *Dissenter in a Great Society.* Nashville: Abingdon Press, 1966.
————. *Free in Obedience.* New York: Seabury Press, 1964.
————. *A Private and Public Faith.* Grand Rapids: Eerdmans, 1962.
————. *An Ethic for Christians and Other Aliens in a Strange Land.* Waco: Word Books, 1973.
Yoder, John Howard. *Politics of Jesus.* Grand Rapids: Eerdmans, 1972.